# The Annunciation to Mary

## A Story of Faith
### Luke 1:26–38

Eugene LaVerdiere, sss

LTP
LITURGY
TRAINING
PUBLICATIONS

To my sister
Claudette LaVerdiere, MM
A woman of Maryknoll

Scripture selections, unless otherwise indicated, are taken from
the *New Revised Standard Version*, copyright 1989, Division
of Christian Education of the National Council of Churches
of Christ in the United States of America.

THE ANNUNCIATION TO MARY: A STORY OF FAITH,
LUKE 1:26–38 © 2004, Archdiocese of Chicago:
Liturgy Training Publications, 1800 North Hermitage Avenue,
Chicago IL 60622-1101; 1-800-933-1800, fax 1-800-933-7094,
e-mail orders@ltp.org. All rights reserved. Website www.ltp.org.

Cover photo © The Crossiers/Gene Plaisted, OSC.

Printed in Canada.

07 06 05 04     5 4 3 2 1

Library of Congress Control Number 2004109932

ISBN 1-56854-557-6
ANNUN

# Contents

༄

*Tables*

# Preface

Thirteen years ago, I went to Japan to give conferences in Kyoto, the old capital of Japan. The city of Kyoto is very large and very beautiful, surrounded by mountains. From the sixth century when it was built until now, Kyoto has never been destroyed.

For one week, I gave conferences on the Eucharist in the New Testament, relating the Eucharist to the universal mission of the Church. After my conferences, I stayed on for an additional week to see the city. I visited many Shinto shrines, Buddhist temples, palaces, and beautiful, contemplative gardens. I walked throughout the city.

Toward the end of the week, I visited the Kyoto National Museum, one of the richest in Japan. This museum's art collection provides a complete panorama, from the Heian Period (AD 794–1192) to the Edo Period (1600–1868).

I saw very beautiful landscape paintings from China, from Korea, and from Japan. But I did not know how to appreciate them. At best, all I could do was mumble to myself, "Beautiful! Beautiful!" I was alone and at this point, I was very tired.

Then, as I stood before a large landscape painting, I noticed a small plaque below the painting that said in Japanese and English: "If you want to appreciate the painting and other landscape paintings, you enter the painting. From the inside, you can see the trees and the mountains around you."

I entered the landscape painting and sat on an enormous rock. From my rock, I saw a path to the mountains. I also saw a stream, and a path crossing the stream by a little arched bridge. There was a pavilion, and inside, a poet drinking tea.

I left my rock, walked along the path, and crossed the stream over the small arched bridge to the pavilion. The poet bowed deeply to me, offering me tea. I very much enjoyed tea with the poet, with whom I conversed for a long time. As I left the pavilion, I bowed very low to the poet, thanking him for the tea and conversation. I then walked on the path high up into the mountains surrounded in mist.

Having entered the landscape painting, I experienced it from the inside for a good two hours, sitting on the big rock, walking on the path, and entering the pavilion. Later, on the steps of the Kyoto National Museum, I was no longer tired. Walking away from the museum, I was extremely excited, thinking of the stories of the Bible from the inside.

Today, I will enter into Luke's story of the Annunciation to Mary and try to experience it from the inside: "In the sixth month the angel Gabriel was sent by God to a town in Galilee called Nazareth, to a virgin engaged to a man whose name was Joseph, of the house of David. The virgin's name was Mary" (Luke 1:26–27).

In offering this book, I wish to thank the members of my family: my parents, Gladys and Laurier; my sister, Sister Claudette, MM; my brother, Brother Gary, SSS, art director–manager of *Emmanuel* magazine; my brother, Peter, his wife, Cheryl, and my nephews, Charles, Kevin, and Jason.

In a special way, I thank my religious family, the Congregation of the Blessed Sacrament, my local community serving St. Jean Baptiste Church in New York, and my provincial superior, Norman Pelletier, SSS, for their constant encouragement and fraternal support.

I also thank Father John E. Kozar, national director of the Society for the Propagation of the Faith, a Pontifical Mission Society, and Monica Ann Yehle, editor of *Mission*, and the entire staff at the National Office for their friendship and support.

I am deeply grateful to my sister Claudette and my classmate Paul Bernier, SSS, editor of *Emmanuel*, for reading the manuscript.

I dedicate this book, *The Annunciation to Mary: A Story of Faith*, to my sister Claudette, a Maryknoll sister. For Maryknoll Sisters, Mary's *Fiat* is enshrined in their congregational motto, "*Ecce Ancilla*

*Domini*, Here am I, the servant of the Lord" (Luke 1:38a). Over the years she has shown me "the servant of the Lord" in Kenya and Tanzania, where she spent more than twenty-five years in mission. After her term as president of the Maryknoll Sisters, she studied Scripture, preparing for a future mission of preaching retreats.

Ecce Ancilla Domini. *Here am I, the servant of the Lord!*
*Eugene La Verdiere, SSS*
*October 18, 2003*
*Feast of St. Luke, Evangelist*

# An Outline
## of Luke 1:26–38

**INTRODUCTION (1:26–27)**
(26) In the sixth month, the angel Gabriel was sent by God
to a town in Galilee called Nazareth, (27) to a virgin engaged
to a man whose name was Joseph, of the house of David.
The virgin's name was Mary.

**BODY (1:28–38A)**
(28a) And he came to her and said,

### Extraordinary Exchanges between Gabriel and Mary:
### In Three Phases

#### First Phase: Angel's Greeting and Mary's Reaction
#### (1:28b–29)

##### Angel's Greeting (28bc)
(28b) "Greetings, favored one! (28c) The Lord is with
you."

##### Mary's Reaction (29ab)
(29a) But she was much perplexed by his words (29b)
and pondered what sort of greeting this might be.

#### Second Phase: Angel's Announcement to Mary and
#### Mary's Question (1:30–34)

##### The Angel Tells Mary What the Greeting is About
##### (1:30–33)
(30) The angel said to her, "Do not be afraid, Mary, for
you have found favor with God. (31) And now, you
will conceive in your womb and bear a son, and you
will name him Jesus. (32) He will be great, and will be
called the Son of the Most High, and the Lord God
will give to him the throne of his ancestor David. (33)

He will reign over the house of Jacob forever, and of his kingdom there will be no end."

### Mary's Question (1:34)

(34) Mary said to the angel, "How can this be, since I am a virgin?"

### Third Phase: Angel's Answer to Mary and Mary's Response (1:35–38a)

### The Angel's Reply to Mary's Question (1:35–37)

(35) The angel said to her, "The Holy Spirit will come upon you, and the power of the Most High will over-shadow you; therefore the child to be born will be holy; he will be called Son of God. (36) And now, your relative Elizabeth in her old age has also con-ceived a son; and this is the sixth month for her who was said to be barren. (37) For nothing will be impossible with God."

### Mary's Response (1:38a)

(38a) Then Mary said, "Here am I, the servant of the Lord; let it be with me according to your word."

## CONCLUSION (1:38B)

(38b) Then the angel departed from her.

# *Praying the Story Together*
# The Annunciation to Mary
## Luke 1:26–38

*Two persons represent the Narrator and the Angel. The rest of the group represent Mary.*

**Narrator:** In the sixth month the angel Gabriel was sent by God to a town in Galilee called Nazareth, to a virgin engaged to a man whose name was Joseph, of the house of David. The virgin's name was Mary. And he came to her and said,

**Angel:** "Greetings, favored one! The Lord is with you."

**Narrator:** But she was much perplexed by his words and pondered what sort of greeting this might be.

The angel said to her,

**Angel:** "Do not be afraid, Mary, for you have found favor with God. And now, you will conceive in your womb and bear a son, and you will name him Jesus. He will be great, and will be called the Son of the Most High, and the Lord God will give him the throne of his ancestor David. He will reign over the house of Jacob forever, and of his kingdom there will be no end."

**Narrator:** But Mary said to the angel,

**Mary:** "How can this be, since I am a virgin?"

**Narrator:** The angel said to her,

**Angel:** "The Holy Spirit will come upon you, and the power of the Most High will overshadow you; therefore the child to be born will be holy; he will be called Son of God.

And now, your relative Elizabeth in her old age has also conceived a son, and this is the sixth month for her who was said to be barren. For nothing will be impossible with God."

**Narrator:** Then Mary said,

**Mary:** "Here am I, the servant of the Lord; let it be with me according to your word."

**Narrator:** Then the angel departed from her.

# Introduction

*The prologue of Luke's Gospel (1:5—2:52)*
*is both simple and profound.*
*Its story of the conception and birth*
*of John the Baptist and of Jesus*
*tells the whole story of Luke-Acts in miniature.*
*One of the prologue's greatest stories*
*is the Annunciation to Mary (1:26–38).*
*To appreciate the richness of the Annunciation*
*and the rest of the prologue we should remember*
*that it was written after, not before,*
*the rest of Luke-Acts.*

Luke is an artist.[1] Luke is also a theologian, an historian, and a superb storyteller. But above all, Luke is a Christian of deep personal faith. In Luke-Acts,[2] all five qualities come together—artist, theologian, historian, storyteller, and person of faith, all in one great story of faith.

Like Paul and the other evangelists, Luke was eager to hand on (*paradidomi*)[3] to others the Gospel he had received (*paralambano*, see 1 Corinthians 11:2, 23; 15:1–3a; 1 Thessalonians 2:13). What Paul did by proclaiming the Gospel, Luke did by telling its story.

In his preface (1:1–4; see Acts 1:1–2) of Luke-Acts, Luke described the Gospel as "an orderly account (*diegesin*, narrative account) of the events that have been fulfilled among us" (Luke 1:1).

He continued, "just as they were handed on (*paredosan*) to us by those who from the beginning were eyewitnesses and servants of the word, I too decided, after investigating everything carefully from the very first, to write an orderly account (*kathexes*, in order) for you, most excellent Theophilus" (1:2–3). Writing the Gospel and Acts, Luke handed on the Gospel to Theophilus[4] and also to us.

As a story of faith, Luke-Acts includes many little stories, each one by itself a wonderful story of faith. In the Gospel, for example, we have the story of the Annunciation to Mary (Luke 1:26–38) and the story of the birth of Jesus in Bethlehem (2:1–20). In the Book of Acts, we have the story of the annunciation to the Apostles in Jerusalem (Acts 1:3–14) and the story of the birth of the Church at Pentecost (2:1–41).

In the Gospel, we also have the story of Martha and Mary (Luke 10:38–42), the story of Zacchaeus (19:1–10), and the story of the disciples of Emmaus (24:13–35). In Acts, we have the story of Peter and John at the Beautiful Gate (Acts 3:1—4:4), the story of the conversion of Saul on the way to Damascus (9:1–31), and the story of Paul addressing the Athenians in the Areopagus at Athens (17:16–34). The list could be very long.

Read separately, each story appears complete in itself. Each little story, however, is only a small unit in Luke's "orderly account of the events that have been fulfilled among us" (Luke 1:1). As such, each story depends on the whole of Luke-Acts for its full meaning, just as Luke-Acts depends on each and every little story for its full meaning. Luke-Acts would not be the same without Martha and Mary, Zacchaeus, the disciples of Emmaus, and the others. Nor would they be the same without their context in Luke-Acts.

One of the most beautiful stories in all of Luke-Acts, indeed in the entire New Testament, is the story of the Annunciation to Mary (1:26–38). Reading the story of the Annunciation to Mary, we have the impression that Luke personally must have seen the

Annunciation as in a vision or a dream, and must have reflected on it for a long time before writing it down.

Toward the end of the story of Jesus' birth, Luke said: "But Mary treasured all these words and pondered them in her heart" (2:19). Describing Mary's response, Luke was speaking from his own personal experience. He too must have kept all these things in his heart. The story of the Annunciation, like the story of Jesus' birth and the other stories in the prologue, is the fruit of Luke's meditation, prayer, and contemplation.

Luke wrote the story of the Annunciation to be read aloud and to be heard. He also wrote it to be seen.[5] According to Greek Christian tradition, Luke was a painter and he is credited with painting the first icon of Our Lady. Even in the West, medieval artists portrayed Luke as a painter. Whether Luke painted with pigments on wood or other solid surfaces, we do not know. But he surely painted with words in the Gospel, and through it on the canvas of the Christian imagination.[6]

The Annunciation to Mary, one of Luke's greatest paintings, challenged translators[7] and interpreters from the very beginning, as it continues to challenge them today, along with preachers, theologians, spiritual writers, indeed, the entire community of faith. It is not surprising that some of the story's greatest interpreters have been artists,[8] representing the Annunciation in frescoes,[9] stained glass,[10] illuminated manuscripts,[11] carved ivories,[12] glazed terra cotta,[13] and engravings.[14] There have been great sculptors also,[15] and painters such as Jan van Eyck,[16] Giotto,[17] Fra Angelico,[18] Fra Filippo Lippi,[19] and El Greco.[20]

The oldest representation of the Annunciation to Mary is the fourth-century fresco on the vault of the cubiculum in the catacomb of Priscilla at Rome. This is the earliest example of what became a most important feature of Christian art. In the fresco, Mary is seated on a throne, and the angel Gabriel is standing, stretching his right arm toward her. Gabriel has no wings, as in the art of this period angels are unwinged.[21]

Every artist presumes that we are familiar with the whole story of the Annunciation. They then select a particular moment and interpret the story from that point of view. Some catch the moment when the angel Gabriel first arrives or when Gabriel is greeting Mary. Some focus on Mary's reaction and show her troubled by Gabriel's greeting. Some show Gabriel anxiously awaiting Mary's response or the virgin Mary giving her *fiat*. Some focus on the very moment of the Incarnation.

In some representations, Gabriel is standing in Mary's presence and Mary is kneeling in prayer. In some, Gabriel is genuflecting before Mary and Mary is standing or seated.

Many artists depict Mary with the Bible open before her on a prie-dieu or in her lap. Sometimes Mary is holding the Bible, open or closed, in her hand. As the angel Gabriel comes to her, Mary is either reading the scriptures or about to read them. The artistic tradition recognizes that Luke's story of the Annunciation is a very biblical story, steeped in biblical history and the word of God. There is no separating the scriptural word from the incarnate Word.

Irenaeus of Lyons reflected the Annunciation to Mary through John's prologue: "and the Word was God" (John 1:1), "And the Word became flesh" (1:14). In *Against Heresies* (5.19–20), he wrote that Mary's obedience reversed Eve's disobedience:

> For as Eve was seduced by the word of an angel to flee from
> God, having rebelled against his Word, so Mary by the word of
> an angel received the glad tidings that she would bear God by
> obeying his Word. The former [Eve] was seduced to disobey God
> and so fell, but the latter [Mary] was persuaded to obey God,
> so that the Virgin Mary might become the advocate of Eve. As the
> human race was subjected to death through the act of a virgin,
> so was it saved by a virgin was precisely balanced by the obedience
> of another.[22]

For many years, Saint Bernard[23] reflected and meditated on the story of the Annunciation to Mary. He preached frequently on this story. In his well-known homily, Saint Bernard imagines the whole world waiting to hear if Mary will say the "yes" on which the outcome of history depends:

> *Behold, Mary, the Angel now awaits your answer. We also, await from your lips the sentence of mercy and compassion. For, the price of our salvation is now offered to you: if you will only consent, we shall at once be set at liberty. Adam, now exiled from paradise with all his miserable offspring, implores this favour of you. For this Abraham entreated you, for this David, for this all the other holy fathers, your own ancestors, who are now dwelling in the shadow of death. See the whole world prostrate at your feet, awaits your answer.*
>
> *For on your word depends the consolation of the desolate, the redemption of the captives, the pardon of the condemned, the salvation of all the children of Adam, of the entire human race.*
>
> *O Virgin do not delay to answer. Speak the word which all on earth, all in limbo, and even all in paradise are waiting to hear. Christ himself, the King and Lord of all, longs for your answer.*
>
> *Make haste, to answer the Angel, or rather to answer the Lord through the Angel. Say the word and receive the Word.*[24]

Saint Bernard contemplated the story of the Annunciation (Luke 1:26–38) through the lens of John's prologue, "In the beginning was the Word, and the Word was with God, and the Word was God" (John 1:1).

Luke's story of the Annunciation has also inspired a mystic and poet like John of the Cross.[25] Here is John of the Cross' *Romance* on the Annunciation to Mary:

1. *Then he called*
   *The archangel Gabriel*
   *And sent him to*
   *The Virgin Mary,*

2. *At whose consent*
   *The mystery was wrought,*
   *In whom the Trinity*
   *Clothed the Word with flesh.*

3. *And though Three work this,*
   *It is wrought in the One:*
   *And the Word lived incarnate*
   *In the womb of Mary.*

4. *And He who had only a Father*
   *Now had a Mother too,*
   *But she was not like others*
   *Who conceived by man.*

5. *From her own flesh*
   *He received His flesh,*
   *So He is called*
   *Son of God and of man.*

John of the Cross viewed Luke's story of the Annunciation through the lens of John's prologue, "In the beginning was the Word. . . . . And the Word became flesh" (John 1:1, 14), and in light of Trinitarian theology.

Cardinal John Henry Newman wrote seven meditations on the Annunciation to Mary in the month of May. He meditated on May 14th on Mary as the Mother of the Creator (*Mater Creatoris*):

> *This is a title [Mother of the Creator] which, of all others, we*
> *should have thought it impossible for any creature to possess.*
> *At first sight we might be tempted to say that it throws into*
> *confusion our primary ideas of the Creator and the creature,*
> *the Eternal and the temporal, the Self-subsisting and the*
> *dependent; and yet on further consideration we shall see that we*

*cannot refuse the title to Mary without denying the Divine*
*Incarnation—that is, the great and fundamental truth*
*of revelation, that God became man.*

*And this was seen as the first age of the Church. Christians*
*were accustomed from the first to call the Blessed Virgin*
*"The Mother of God," because they say that it was impossible*
*to deny her that title without denying St. John's words,*
*"The Word" (that is, God the Son) "was made flesh."*[26]

Like Saint Irenaeus, Saint Bernard, and Saint John of the Cross, John
Henry Newman meditated on the Annunciation to Mary through
the lens of John's prologue.

We can view the story of the Annunciation as an icon, a narrative icon, filled with God's truth and goodness. The principal figure in the icon is the virgin Mary, herself a personal icon of the
Church. In *Lumen Gentium*, Vatican II presented her as such:

*In the meantime the Mother of Jesus in the glory which she*
*possesses in body and soul in heaven is the image (in Latin,*
imago; *in Greek* eikon) *and beginning of the Church as*
*it is to be perfected in the world to come. Likewise she shines*
*forth on earth, until the day of the Lord shall come (cf. 2 Pet*
*3:10), a sign of certain hope and comfort to the pilgrim People*
*of God."*[27]

As an icon, the story of the Annunciation invites and draws us into
its mystery. It invites us to contemplative communion with Gabriel,
the angel sent from God, and with Mary, the virgin who conceived
the Son of God. It puts us in touch with Gabriel's greeting to Mary
and the announcement of Jesus' conception and birth, as well as
with Mary's response: "Here am I, the servant of the Lord; let it be
with me according to your word" (Luke 1:38).

Gabriel's message to Mary contains an extraordinary Christological synthesis. Jesus is the Son of the Most High, who would receive the throne of David his ancestor and who would reign over the house of Jacob forever (1:32–33). Conceived by the Holy Spirit, he would be called holy, the Son of God (1:35). Mary's response epitomizes the vocation of the Church in relation to the Incarnation. The whole Church, indeed every Christian, is called to conceive and bring forth the Son of God into the world.[28] In Luke's story of the Annunciation to Mary, truth and goodness are borne on the wings of beauty.

The story of the Annunciation to Mary (1:26–38) is read in seven Masses of the liturgical year:

1. The Fourth Sunday of Advent (Year B, the liturgical year of Mark),

2. December 20 (the weekday of Advent),

3. The Annunciation of the Lord (March 25),

4. The Queenship of the Blessed Virgin Mary (August 22),

5. Our Lady of the Rosary (October 7),

6. The Immaculate Conception of the Blessed Virgin Mary (December 8), and

7. Our Lady of Guadalupe (December 12).

It is read in the Masses in the Common of the Blessed Virgin Mary as the fourth choice and in the Ritual Mass of the Consecration of Virgins and Religious Profession as the ninth choice.

The Annunciation to Mary (1:26–38) is read in more Masses in the liturgical year than any other of the stories in Luke-Acts.

## Narrative Structure

Like most great stories, the story of the Annunciation has a very simple narrative structure, beginning with the introduction (1:26–27), continuing with the body (1:28–38a), and ending with the conclusion (1:38b).

The introduction situates the story in time and place and presents the story's two personages, the angel Gabriel and the virgin Mary. It was in the sixth month when the angel Gabriel was sent from God to a city in Galilee named Nazareth, to a virgin engaged (*emnesteumenen*) to a man named Joseph, who was of the house of David. The virgin's name was Mary (1:26–27).

The body consists of a dialogue between the angel Gabriel and the virgin Mary (1:28–38). It begins with the angel's arrival: "And he came to her (*kai eiselthon pros auten*) and said" (1:28a). It ends with the angel's departure: "Then (*kai*) the angel departed from her (*apelthen ap' autes*)" (1:38b). The dialogue between Gabriel and Mary unfolds in three distinct but closely related phases:

1. the angel's greeting and Mary's reaction (1:28b–29);

2. the angel's announcement and Mary's question (1:30–34);

3. the angel's answer and Mary's response (1:35–38a).

In the first phase, the dialogue opens with the angel's greeting: "Greetings (*chaire*, hail), favored one (*kecharitomene*, singularly or fully graced)! The Lord is with you." The story then describes Mary's reaction. Mary was much perplexed, or deeply troubled, at the greeting and pondered what it meant (1:28–29).

The first phase, with the angel's greeting and Mary's reaction, brings us to the very heart of the story, an extraordinary exchange between Gabriel, the one who was sent from God, and Mary, the virgin of Nazareth. This exchange unfolds in the dialogue's second and third phases (1:30–38a).

In the second phase (1:30–34), the angel Gabriel tells Mary not to fear. She has found grace before God. The angel then tells Mary what the extraordinary greeting was about. Mary the virgin, the one singularly or fully graced, would conceive in her womb, bring forth a son, and name him Jesus. Her son would be called the Son of the Most High and would be given the throne of David his father (1:30–33).

Responding to the announcement, Mary then asks the most crucial question in Luke's Gospel, perhaps in the entire New Testament: "How can this (*touto*) be, since I am a virgin?" or more literally, "since I do not know (*ou ginosko*) man?" (1:34).

In the third phase (1:35–38a), the angel tells Mary how "this" (*touto*) would be, that is, how Mary would conceive the one who will be called the Son of the Most High: "The Holy Spirit will come upon you, and the power of the Most High will overshadow you" (1:35a). That is how Mary would conceive the Son of the Most High, not through any human effort or relationship but through the Holy Spirit. The angel then gives Mary a sign, showing that nothing is impossible for God. Elizabeth, Mary's relative, has conceived in her old age and is already in her sixth month (1:35–37).

The third phase, and with it the whole dialogue between the angel Gabriel and Mary, concludes with Mary's response. Mary, graced as she was, accepts Gabriel's extraordinary announcement and declares herself totally at God's disposition: "Here am I, the servant (*doule*) of the Lord; let it be (*fiat*) with me according to your word" (1:38a).

The conclusion of the story coincides with the end of the dialogue: "Then the angel departed from her" (1:38b). The angel Gabriel had been sent from God to a virgin whose name was Mary (1:26–27). Coming to her with an extraordinary greeting (1:28) and an even more extraordinary announcement (1:31–33, 35–37), the angel departed from her after receiving Mary's response (1:38b).

# Context in Prologue

As part of Luke's prologue (1:5—2:52), the Annunciation to Mary (1:26–38) presents some of the most basic themes of Luke-Acts. Like the prologues for the other Gospels (Mark 1:2–13; Matthew 1:1–2:23; John 1:1–18; Acts 1:3–14), Luke's prologue can be described as "the Gospel in miniature." The story of the Annunciation is a very important part of Luke's "Gospel in miniature."

Luke began the prologue with another annunciation story, in which the angel Gabriel appeared to Zechariah and announced the conception and birth of John the Baptist (1:5–25). After the two annunciation stories, the prologue tells how Mary, now pregnant with Jesus, visited her relative Elizabeth, already pregnant with John the Baptist.

*An Outline of Luke's Prologue*
*Luke 1:5—2:52*

I. Jesus in His Ultimate Origins 1:5—2:40
   A. Annunciations and Visitation 1:5–56
      1. The annunciation to Zechariah 1:5–25
      2. The Annunciation to Mary 1:26–38
      3. Mary visits Elizabeth 1:39–56
   B. Manifestations and Presentation 1:57–2:40
      1. The birth of John the Baptist 1:57–80
      2. The birth of Jesus 2:1–21
      3. The presentation in the temple 2:22–40
II. Jesus in His Ultimate Destiny 2:41–52

The prologue continues with the stories of the birth and the naming of John the Baptist (1:57–80) and of Jesus (2:1–21). After the two birth stories, it tells how Jesus was presented to the Lord at the temple in Jerusalem (2:22–40). The prologue concludes with the story of how Jesus accompanied his parents to Jerusalem for Passover (2:41–52). At the time, Jesus was about twelve years old (2:42).

Like the prologue for the Gospel of Matthew (Matthew 1:1—2:23), Luke's prologue is often called "an infancy narrative."[29] But the two prologues are quite different. Matthew tells the story of the infancy from the point of view of Joseph. Luke tells the story from the point of view of Mary. As the Gospel of the kingdom of heaven, Matthew stresses royal personages and events connected with the history of the kingdom. As the Gospel of prophetic fulfillment, Luke stresses prophetic personages and events connected with prophetic history.

Luke's prologue is noted for its parallel stories.[30] In terms of religious art, we may think of them as *diptychs*. First, we have the announcement diptych, with the annunciation to Zechariah on the left (1:5–25) and the Annunciation to Mary on the right (1:26–38).

*An Outline of the Diptychs*

I.   The Diptych of the Annunciation  1:5–38
    A.   The annunciation to Zechariah:
         the conception of John the Baptist  1:5–25
    B.   The Annunciation to Mary:
         the conception of Jesus  1:26–38
II.  The Diptych of the Birth  1:57—2:21
    A.   The birth of John the Baptist  1:57–80
    B.   The birth of Jesus  2:1–21

Later, we have the birth diptych, with the birth of John the Baptist on the left (1:57–80) and the birth of Jesus on the right (2:1–21).

In both diptychs, Luke shows how Jesus is related to John. At the same time, he shows how Jesus is far superior to John. John will be called the prophet of the Most High (1:76a). Jesus will be called the Son of the Most High (1:32). John was filled with the Holy Spirit from his mother's womb (1:15, 44). Jesus was conceived by the Holy Spirit (1:35). John will go before the Lord to prepare his way (1:76b). Jesus is a savior who is Christ and Lord (2:11), the one whose way John would prepare.

Each diptych is followed by a complementary story. For the annunciation diptych, we have the story of the Visitation (1:39–56), in which John the Baptist is quickened by the Holy Spirit in a pre-natal encounter with Jesus. For the births, we have the story of the Presentation of Jesus in the temple (2:22–40), in which Jesus and his parents fulfill the law of the Lord as well as prophetic expectation.

In terms of religious art, we may also think of the two sets of stories as *triptychs*. The first triptych includes the annunciation of the birth of John the Baptist on the left (1:5–25), and the Visitation on the right (1:39–56). In this first triptych, the Annunciation of the birth of Jesus is in the center (1:26–38).

The second triptych includes the birth of John the Baptist on the left (1:57–80), and the Presentation in the temple on the right (2:22–40). In this second triptych, the birth of Jesus is in the center (2:1–21).

With its story of the Visitation, the first triptych (1:5–56) shows how Jesus and John are related in the history of salvation. Jesus' messianic mission fulfills the promise of John's prophetic mission. With its story of the Presentation in the temple, the second triptych (1:57—2:40) shows how Jesus is superior to John. Jesus is directly related to the temple, God's earthly dwelling, the place of God's presence in the city of David.

*An Outline of the Triptychs*

I.  The Triptych of the Annunciation  1:5–56
    A.  The annunciation to Zechariah  1:5–25
    B.  The Annunciation to Mary  1:26–38
    C.  Mary visits Elizabeth  1:39–56
II. The Triptych of the Birth  1:57—2:40
    A.  The birth of John the Baptist  1:57–80
    B.  The birth of Jesus  2:1–21
    C.  The Presentation in the temple  2:22–40

Jesus' mission represents a radically new era in the history of salvation. John's mission was to the children of Israel (1:16). Jesus' mission was to "all people, a light for revelation to the Gentiles and for glory to your people Israel" (2:31–32). John's mission was related to the mission of Israel as a people of God set apart. Jesus' mission was related to the mission of the Church gathering all peoples as a people of God.

The parallelism of the two triptychs are surely part of the structure of the prologue. But after the birth triptych (1:57—2:40), the prologue continues with an additional story about a journey to Jerusalem for Passover (2:41–52), breaking the prologue's literary symmetry. Several indications suggest that this Passover story was added after the rest of the prologue was written.

The story of the Presentation in the temple ends with a summary of Jesus' growth and development: "The child grew and became strong, filled with wisdom; and the favor (*charis*) of God was upon him" (2:40). The summary parallels an earlier summary of the growth and development of John the Baptist: "The child grew and became strong in spirit, and he was in the wilderness until the day he appeared publicly to Israel" (1:80). Concluding the first and third panels of the triptych, the summaries and their respective stories frame the central panel portraying the birth and manifestation of Jesus.

As a pendant to the summary of the growth and development of John the Baptist (1:80), that of Jesus' growth and development (2:40) concludes the birth triptych (1:57—2:40). At the same time, it concludes the entire prologue from the annunciation to Zechariah to the Presentation of Jesus in the temple (1:5—2:40).

But then at the end of the Passover story, we find another concluding summary, modeled on the previous summary: "And Jesus increased in wisdom and in years, and in divine and human favor (*chariti*)" (2:52). This second concluding summary must have been added when Luke broke the prologue's carefully planned symmetry and added the story of Jesus' journey to Jerusalem for Passover (2:41–52). As a result, the expanded prologue was given a new literary structure.

Like the earlier structure, the new is in two parts. The first part includes the whole prologue as originally planned with its two triptychs (1:5—2:40). This first part, with the Annunciation and birth triptychs, presents who Jesus is from the point of view of Jesus' ultimate origins. The second part, with its story of Jesus' journey to Jerusalem for Passover, is very short but no less significant. This second part presents who Jesus is from the point of view of Jesus' ultimate destiny. "Did you not know that I must (dei) be in my Father's house?" (2:49).

The second part of the prologue (2:41–52) tells about Jesus' journey to Jerusalem for the feast of Passover. For the journey, Jesus traveled with his parents, the people who were closest to him at the time. After celebrating the feast, his parents lost him and searched for him everywhere. Returning to Jerusalem, they found him on the third day in the temple, listening to the teachers and answering questions. His mother said to him: "Son, why have you done this to us? Your father and I have been looking for you with great anxiety" (2:48). In response, Jesus asked: "Why were you searching for me? Did you not know that I must (dei) be in my Father's house?" (2:49).

The story parallels Jesus' great journey to Jerusalem, the place where he would be taken up to heaven to be with his Father (9:51—24:53). For the journey, Jesus was accompanied by his followers, those who were closest to him at that time (9:52–62). On the way to the Ascension (24:50–53), Jesus and his disciples would celebrate a definitive Passover in which they would lose him in the Passion and find him on the third day. The story of Emmaus (24:13–35) shows Jesus listening to the disciples and responding to them (24:19b–27). So does the story of the Ascension in the prologue of Acts (Acts 1:3–14).[31]

The added story transforms the literary structure of the prologue. The original structure, with its two triptychs, was very symmetrical. The new structure, with the additional story, is not. The first part includes the whole of the original prologue, with its two triptychs and their focus on Jesus' ultimate origins (Luke 1:5—2:40). The second part includes the journey to Jerusalem for Passover, with its focus on Jesus' ultimate destiny (2:41–52). The two parts complement one another, presenting the basic themes of Luke-Acts in terms of Jesus' origins and destiny.

The Annunciation to Mary is told in the first part of the prologue, where it makes a major contribution to the story of Jesus' ultimate origins. In that first part, the Annunciation to Mary occupies the central panel in the annunciation triptych and it must be read in relation to the annunciation to Zechariah and the Visitation.

The Annunciation is also closely related to the story of Jesus' birth, which occupies the corresponding panel in the birth triptych. Gabriel's announcement of Jesus' conception and birth is the prologue's first major statement regarding Jesus and his mission. As such it gives the basis for the second major statement given in the story of Jesus' birth (2:1–20). The story of the Annunciation and the story of Jesus' birth must be read in relation to one another.

As part of the story of Jesus' ultimate origins (1:5—2:40), the Annunciation is also related to the story of Jesus' ultimate destiny (2:41–52). Jesus, the Son of the Most High, must return to his Father. As the bondservant (*doule*) of the Lord, Mary accepts to be the mother of God's Son. In that, she also accepts her son's Passion, Resurrection, and Ascension.

## Beginning of Luke-Acts

To appreciate the Annunciation to Mary, we have to view it in the context of the whole prologue (1:5—2:52). We also have to view it in the context of the beginning of Luke-Acts (1:1—4:13). Luke-Acts opens with a preface (1:1–4), continues with the prologue (1:5—2:52), and concludes with a section devoted to the background and preparation for the mission of Jesus (3:1—4:13). Reading Luke's Gospel from the beginning, we have the impression that the Gospel begins over and over again before Jesus' mission is introduced in 4:14–44.

There are good reasons to believe that when Luke-Acts was first written, it did not have an infancy narrative as a prologue (1:5—2:52). As first written, Luke's prologue was what we now describe as a section devoted to the background and preparation for Jesus' mission (3:1—4:13). This original prologue focused on the origins of Jesus' mission and associated Jesus' divinity with his baptism. The new prologue focused on the ultimate origins of Jesus and associated his divinity with his very conception.[32]

*An Outline of the Original Prologue*
*Luke 3:1—4:13*

I.   The mission of John the Baptist (3:1–20) (Mark 1:2–8)
II.  The baptism of Jesus (3:21–22) (Mark 1:9–11)
III. The genealogy of Jesus (3:23–38) (Matthew 1:1–17)
IV.  The temptations of Jesus (4:1–13) (Mark 1:12–13)

Luke's new prologue (1:5—2:52) was written after the rest of Luke-Acts, including the original prologue (3:1—4:13), had been completed. The new prologue represents Luke's effort to provide a better introduction for "the events that have been fulfilled among us" (1:1).[33] The addition of the new prologue moved Luke-Acts into its second edition.

In that new edition, the new prologue, the infancy narrative with its story of the Annunciation to Mary, displaced the original prologue to a secondary position. We may consider the new prologue as a further and deeper reflection on John's preparatory mission (3:1–20), Jesus' baptism (3:21–22), Jesus' biblical origins as told in the genealogy (3:23–38), and Jesus' victory over every test (4:1–13). As such, the story of the Annunciation to Mary is part of Luke's most mature reflection on "the events that have been fulfilled among us" (1:1).

The indications that Luke wrote the infancy narrative after the rest of Luke-Acts can be treated under three headings, including the preface of Luke-Acts (1:1–4), the secondary preface of the Acts of the Apostles (1:1–2), and the relationship of Luke 3:1—4:13 to Mark 1:1–13 and Matthew 1:1–17.

*The Preface of Luke-Acts (Luke 1:1–4)*

Luke-Acts opens with a short preface (1:1–4), in which Luke relates his work to previous efforts and gives his purpose for writing.[34] A close look at this preface indicates that Luke very likely planned to begin the Gospel with Jesus' adult mission.

Like many before him, Luke undertook "to set down an orderly account of the events that have been fulfilled among us" (1:1). Like his precedessors, Luke handed on what had been handed down by those who were "eyewitnesses and servants of the word" (1:2).

Writing in the 80s, some five decades after the events, Luke investigated "everything accurately from the very first" and wrote it down "in an orderly account" (1:3) so that Theophilus might "know the truth concerning the things about which you have been instructed" (1:4). Through Theophilus, Luke addressed Christian communities that were heir to Paul's missionary preaching, beginning with the church at Antioch. At the time Luke wrote, Christianity was in its third generation.

Since Luke sought to show the certainty of the teachings which Theophilus and others received, Luke must have noted some uncertainty in the faith of Christians. His research into the tradition and his presentation of it in an "orderly account" were meant to address that uncertainty.

We should, therefore, read the whole of Luke-Acts in light of Luke's intention to strengthen the faith of Christians concerning Jesus and his role in the history of salvation. With its focus on Jesus' identity and mission, the Annunciation story would eventually contribute greatly to that effort.

Those who were eyewitnesses from the beginning handed on what they saw as witnesses in their ministry of the word. Who were those eyewitnesses? What did Luke mean in the expression, "from the beginning"?

First, note that Luke referred to "those who from the beginning were eyewitnesses (*autoptai*)," not to those who were witnesses (*martyres*). The eyewitnesses were there at the beginning of Jesus' ministry. They became witnesses and began their ministry of the word at Pentecost (see Luke 24:48–49; Acts 1:8).[35]

Not every eyewitness (*autoptes*) became Jesus' witness (*martys*). The difference is spelled out in Peter's qualifications for the choice of Judas' successor: "So one of the men who have accompanied us during all the time that the Lord Jesus went in and out among us, beginning from the baptism of John until the day when he was taken up from us," that is, one who was an eyewitness (*autoptes*), "become with us a witness (*martys*) to his resurrection" (Acts 1:21–22).

To be a witness with the apostles, someone had to be an eyewitness from the beginning. The witness, therefore, which began with Pentecost, was inseparable from the whole of Jesus' ministry as prepared by the baptism of John. But according to Peter, it did not include the infancy narrative.

## The Secondary Preface of the Acts of the Apostles (*Acts 1:1–2*)

The secondary preface of the Acts of the Apostles summarizes Luke's first book as dealing with "all that Jesus did and taught from the beginning until the day when he was taken up to heaven, after giving instructions through the Holy Spirit to the apostles whom he had chosen" (Acts 1:1–2). As did Peter in Acts 1:21–22, the preface describes the Gospel as beginning with Jesus' ministry, not with Jesus' conception and birth.

Peter did the same in Caesarea in a summary of Jesus' life while addressing the household of Cornelius: "You know the message he sent to the people of Israel, preaching peace by Jesus Christ—he is Lord of all. That message spread throughout Judea, beginning in Galilee after the baptism that John announced . . . " (Acts 10:36–37). When Luke wrote the preface of Acts[36] and these other summaries of Jesus' life and ministry, he did not plan to include an infancy narrative.

The preface of Acts, therefore, with its summary of the Gospel, indicates that Luke-Acts most probably had two successive editions. The first edition did not include the infancy narrative (1:5—2:52). But that does not mean that the first edition was without a prologue. After the preface (1:1–4), the original prologue presented the ministry of John the Baptist, the baptism of Jesus, the genealogy of Jesus, and the three great tests in the desert (3:1—4:13).[37] The second edition included the infancy narrative as a new prologue.

*The Title and Prologue of Mark's Gospel (Mark 1:1–13)*

A comparison between the title (Mark 1:1) and the prologue of Mark (1:2–13) shows that Luke most probably wrote 3:1—4:13 as a prologue for Luke-Acts.

Mark provided a basic source for Luke and was surely one of those who had "undertaken to set down an orderly account of the events that have been fulfilled among us" (Luke 1:1). For Mark, "the beginning of the good news of Jesus Christ, the Son of God" (Mark 1:1) referred to the whole of Mark's Gospel. Mark's story of "the beginning of the good news" began with a prologue, telling about the mission and ministry of John the Baptist (1:2–8), the baptism of Jesus (1:9–11), and Jesus' forty-day test in the desert (1:12–13).

What we now describe as the background and preparation for Jesus' mission (Luke 3:1—4:13) is clearly based on Mark's prologue

(1:2–13). Following Mark's prologue, Luke wrote a prologue for Luke-Acts, beginning with the mission and ministry of John the Baptist (3:1–20; see Mark 1:2–8), the baptism of Jesus (3:21–22; see Mark 1:9–11), and ending with Jesus' forty-day test in the desert (4:1–13; see Mark 1:12–13). Between the baptism of Jesus and the forty-day test, he inserted a genealogy of Jesus (3:23–38).

As we see from Matthew's genealogy (1:1–17), early Christians found that a genealogy of Jesus made an important contribution to a prologue.[38] Matthew used a genealogy to introduce his infancy narrative. In his original prologue, Luke used a genealogy (3:23–38) to relate God's beloved Son (3:21–22) to biblical history.

In relation to the beginning of Luke-Acts (1:1—4:13), the Annunciation to Mary is part of Luke's new prologue. In the original prologue (3:1—4:13), Mary was not even mentioned.

Christologically, the original prologue focused on the descent of the Holy Spirit and the heavenly voice declaring Jesus the beloved Son of God; on Jesus' genealogy reaching back to Adam, the son of God; and on Jesus' response to the triple temptation, showing him human as well as divine. Like the new prologue, the old tells about Jesus' identity and mission, but in terms of his historical and biblical origins. The only hint concerning Jesus' ultimate origins came in the genealogy: "Jesus was about thirty years old when he began his work. He was the son (as was thought, *hos enomizeto*) of Joseph" (3:23).

In the new prologue, the Christology focuses on the conception, the birth, and the naming of Jesus, his Presentation in the temple, and his Passover journey to the temple. Unlike the original prologue, the new prologue tells about Jesus' ultimate origins and Jesus' ultimate destiny. What was in the original prologue but a hint concerning Jesus' true parentage is developed in the story of the Annunciation to Mary, showing how Jesus was conceived through the Holy Spirit.

As a figure of the Church, Mary brings an ecclesiological dimension to the new prologue. The original prologue focused on Christology. The new focuses on both Christology and ecclesiology. Announcing Jesus' conception and birth, the story of the Annunciation is a Christological statement. Commissioning Mary to conceive in her womb and give birth to Jesus, it is also an ecclesiological statement.

## Literary Form

The literary form of the Annunciation is fairly complex, integrating several forms from biblical literature and adapting them to the unique story of the Annunciation to Mary.[39] In writing the Annunciation, Luke knew and respected the traditional forms. Using those forms, he evoked several biblical stories and prophetic announcements, giving the story of the Annunciation scriptural depth and biblical resonance. Even the most creative writer or artist works within a tradition.

While working within a tradition, Luke used the literary forms very creatively, giving the story of the Annunciation a unique form and structure. The story of the Annunciation to Mary may have relatives in the Old and New Testaments, but no peers. There is no story in all of biblical literature quite like the Annunciation to Mary.

Interpreting the story, we must examine the literary forms that guided the author. But in doing that, we must not reduce the story to a common denominator. Examining the literary forms in the story of the Annunciation, we must attend to the story's uniqueness.

In writing the story, Luke followed three basic literary forms, well-known from the Old Testament. The first and most basic is that of the announcement of a birth. The second is that of the broader story in which a birth is announced. The third is the form of a commission or election story. All three are integrated in Luke's story of the Annunciation to Mary.[40]

### The Announcement of a Birth

At the core of the story (1:31–33), we have the traditional form of the announcement of a birth. The form includes four distinct but closely related elements, all present in the Annunciation to Mary:

1. the particle "behold," in Greek, *idou* (v. 31a), introducing
2. the conception and birth of the child (v. 31b) and
3. the naming of the child (v. 31c);
4. the identity and historic mission of the child (vv. 32–33).

In the Old Testament, we find the same four elements in the same order in the announcement of the birth of Ishmael (Genesis 16:11–12)[41] and in the announcement of the birth of Isaac (17:19),[42] both of which belong to the priestly tradition (P). We also find the same form in Isaiah's oracle concerning the birth of Immanuel, where the identity of the child coincides with his name: "God is with us" (Isaiah 7:14; see Matthew 1:23). Except for the naming of the child, three of the elements are also present in the announcement of the birth of Samson (Judges 13:3–5).

In the New Testament, we find the same elements in Matthew in the announcement of Jesus' birth (Matthew 1:20–21), but without the introductory particle, "behold" (1:21; but see 1:23). In Luke, we find the same elements for the announcement of the birth of John the Baptist (Luke 1:13–17), but again without the introductory particle, "behold" (1:13).

Later in Luke, the same basic elements are present in the announcement of Jesus' birth to the shepherds, where the particle "behold" is present (2:10), but the child's name is not announced. In its place, we have two Christological titles, Messiah (Christ) and Lord, closely associated with the child's salvific mission: "For see (*idou*)—I am bringing you good news of great joy for all the people: to you is born this day in the city of David a Savior, who is the Messiah, the Lord" (Luke 2:10–11).

### The Announcement Story

The literary form of the announcement itself (1:31–33) is integrated into the larger story of the Annunciation to Mary. That larger form has a much looser literary pattern than the actual announcement. It includes a general set of elements but not in the same order. In the Old Testament, we find those elements especially in the announcement of the birth of Isaac (Genesis 17) and the announcement of the birth of Samson (Judges 13). But we do not find them in the announcement of the birth of Ishmael (Genesis 16)[43] or in Isaiah's prophetic announcement of the conception and birth of Immanuel (Isaiah 7:14; see Matthew 1:21).

Here are the five principal elements of the literary form for an announcement story, as applied to the Annunciation to Mary:

1. the appearance of an angel, the angel of the Lord, or the Lord Himself (Luke 1:26–28a);

2. a reaction of fear, reverence, or sacred awe (1:29);

3. the announcement of the birth, including the conception, the name, and the role (1:31–33);

4. an objection from the one who receives the announcement, or in the case of Mary, a simple question (1:34);

5. and a sign given by the angel (1:36).

At the heart of the announcement story is the actual announcement of the birth. Most of the other elements are present in each of the stories but not in the same order. In the New

Testament, the first three elements are present in Matthew's annunciation to Joseph (Matthew 1:20–21). All five are present in Luke's annunciation to Zechariah (Luke 1:11–20). Except for the fourth element, the objection or question, they are also present in the annunciation to the shepherds (2:8–12).

Some of the elements vary considerably from story to story, in both content and context. If we did not have the Lukan stories announcing the birth of John the Baptist (1:5–25) and of Jesus (1:26–38), I suspect we would not speak of a special literary form for stories announcing the birth of a child. It is while analyzing the Lukan stories and exploring their Old Testament background that we discern the general pattern with the five elements.

The pattern allows us to associate the Annunciation to Mary with the literary form, at least loosely, but at the same time we have to recognize the individuality of each story, including the story of the Annunciation. Some of the elements in the Annunciation to Mary may parallel elements in the other stories but they also differ considerably. For example, for the announcement of Isaac's birth, the Lord himself appears to Abraham (Genesis 17:1). For the announcement of Samson's birth, "the angel of the Lord," an expression equivalent to the Lord Himself,[44] appears to the wife of Manoah and to her husband (Judges 13:3). In the Annunciation to Mary, the angel Gabriel was sent from God (Luke 1:26–27) and came to Mary (1:28a).

Abraham prostrated himself before God (Genesis 17:3, 17). Reporting the appearance to her husband, the wife of Manoah described that a man came to her, one whose "appearance was like that of an angel of God, most awe-inspiring" (Judges 13:6; see also 13:20). In the case of Abraham and the wife of Manoah, the fear or awe was inspired by the appearance of God or by one with the appearance of an angel of God. Mary, on the other hand, was troubled not by the angel's appearance but by the angel's greeting.

Like Zechariah, Mary asks a question of the angel Gabriel, but unlike Zechariah, she does not object to Gabriel's announcement. Zechariah's question came from his lack of faith. Mary's question was prompted by faith.

Note that in the stories of the announcement of the birth of Isaac (Genesis 17) and of Samson (Judges 13) there is no greeting (compare Luke 1:28) and no verbal response from the one who receives the announcement (compare Luke 1:38). Note also that Mary's question (1:34) invites a further elaboration of the announcement (1:35).

### The Commission Story

In the Annunciation to Mary, the announcement of the birth is presented as an integral part, indeed the very heart, of the greater story announcing the birth. In turn, the story announcing the birth is integrated into a commission story.[45]

For the form of the announcement story, we had the Old Testament stories of the conception and birth of Isaac (Genesis 17) and of Samson (Judges 13). For the form of the commission story, we have the Old Testament stories of the commission of Abraham (Genesis 11:28–30; 12:1–4a; 15:1–6), Isaac (26:1–6; 26:23–25), Jacob (28:10–22; 35:9–15; 46:1–5a), Joseph (41:37–45), Moses (Exodus 3:1—4:16; 6:2–13; 7:1–6), Gideon (Judges 6:11–24), and many others.[46] Like the greater story announcing the birth, the form of a commissioning story follows a loose pattern. It includes several elements but not always in the same order.

The form of a commissioning story includes seven elements, all present in the Annunciation to Mary:

1. an introduction, introducing the personages and the setting (Luke 1:26–27);

2. a confrontation, including a greeting (1:28);

3. a troubled reaction (1:29);

4. the actual commission, in which the one commissioned is addressed by name (1:30);

5. a protest, objection, or question (1:34);

6. a reassurance or response to the question (1:35–37);

7. a conclusion, including the response of the one commissioned (1:38).

The announcement of the conception and birth (1:31–33) is integral to the annunciation pattern but is not part of the commission pattern. On the other hand, the opening greeting (1:28) and the response (1:38) are not part of the annunciation pattern but are integral to the commission pattern.

Note that in Luke's story of the Annunciation, the fourth element, that is, the actual commission (1:30), is not stressed. The angel responds to Mary's fear, addresses her by name, and then refers back to the greeting. Mary has found favor (*charis*, grace) before God. Mary's commission is assumed. That she would accept the word of Gabriel and be the servant (*doule*) of the Lord is never in doubt. The commission of Mary, therefore, is completely subordinate to the announcement of Jesus' conception and birth.

In theological terms, the role of Mary, the first of the believers, the first Christian disciple, and the mother of Jesus, is relative to her son, the Son of God. The ecclesiology in the story of the Annunciation to Mary is subordinate to the Christology, and not vice versa.

---

1. In the introduction of *Luke: Artist and Theologian*, Robert J. Karris says, "I contend that Luke's artistry is a vehicle for his theology" (New York: Paulist Press, 1985), 1.

2. Unlike Mark, Matthew, and John, Luke told the story of the Gospel in two volumes, the Gospel according to Luke and the Acts of the Apostles. For Luke,

the story of the Church was part of the Gospel. Luke's Gospel introduces the Church in the Acts of the Apostles. To highlight the thematic unity of Luke's two-volume work, we shall refer to it as Luke-Acts.

3. Paul used the terms "to receive" (*paralambano*) and "to hand on" (*paradidomi*), reflecting the technical language of Jewish rabbinic tradition (1 Corinthians 11:2, 23; 15:1–3a; 1 Thessalonians 2:13). The rabbis used the equivalent Hebrew verbs, *qibbel* ("to receive") and *masar* ("to hand on"), having virtually a technical meaning. See Raymond F. Collins, *First Corinthians*, Sacra Pagina 7 (Collegeville: The Liturgical Press, 1999), 425–426 and notes 11:23 and 15:1–3.

   See also Jacob Neusner, *The Mishnah, A New Translation* (New Haven: Yale University Press, 1988), Fourth Division, *Abot* ("Fathers"):

   > (*1:1*) *"Moses received Torah at Sinai and handed it on to Joshua, Joshua to elders, and elders to prophets. The prophets handed it on to the men of the great assembly. . . . (1:12) Hillel and Shammai (c. 30 BC–AD 10) received [it] from them."* 672–674

   Saul Paul in Jerusalem was a student of the great teacher, Rabban Gamaliel (*Abot* 1:16), the grandson or son of Hillel: "I am a Jew, born in Tarsus in Cilicia, but brought up in this city (Jerusalem) at the feet of Gamaliel, educated strictly according to our ancestral law, being zealous for God, just as all of you are today" (Acts 22:3; see 5:34–39).

4. Theophilus (1:3; Acts 1:1; in Greek, *Theophilos*, meaning "beloved of God") was probably Luke's influential patron or a personal symbol of Luke's readers: "Perhaps Luke's patron; he is also representative of a wider audience which needs upbuilding in faith," Robert J. Karris, OFM, "The Gospel according to Luke," Raymond E. Brown, SS, Joseph A. Fitzmyer, SJ, and Roland E. Murphy, OCARM, eds., *The New Jerome Biblical Commentary* (Englewood Cliffs, N.J.: Prentice-Hall, 1990, 1968), 678.

5. For Luke, the Gospel had to be seen as well as heard. The shepherds, for example, wanted to see what had been made known to them (2:15; see also 2:17). And when messengers came to Jesus from John the Baptist asking, "Are you the one who is to come, or are we to wait for another?" (7:19–20). Jesus answered, "Go and tell John what you have seen and heard . . ." (7:22; see 7:18–23).

6. Luke is very visual in his writing, and this may the source of the tradition that he was an artist. Luke may not have painted with pigments, but he surely painted with words, inviting Christian artists to take up his word pictures and present them in every medium.

7. Luke's story of the Annunciation (1:26–38) is filled with allusions to scripture. Its evocative language, delicate nuances, and levels of meaning make it extremely difficult to translate. Its many translations, both ancient and modern, parallel the history of its interpretation down to our own time.

8. In *Mary through the Centuries: Her Place in the History of Culture*, Jaroslav Pelikan says, "If historians of art or of the church were to follow the example of their colleagues in the natural sciences by compiling a 'citation index,' not of the articles, papers, and books of other scholars as scientists do, but of the themes that have captured the attention of painters and sculptors throughout history, and especially if they were to prepare such an index together, it seems clear that among all the scenes in the life of the Virgin Mary that have engaged the piety of the devout and the creativity of the artists, the annunciation has been predominant. The annunciation has been so prevalent, in fact, that the number of references to it in such an index would probably exceed the number of references to all other Marian themes combined" (New Haven: Yale University Press, 1996), 81. Pelikan's book includes 18 illustrations, representing the Annunciation in various forms.

9. The oldest fresco of the Annunciation is a fourth-century fresco on the vault of the cubiculum in the catacomb of Priscilla in Rome. For a photo of the fresco, see Jaroslav Pelikan, *Mary through the Centuries*, first illustration between pages 84 and 85.

10. One of the finest representations in stained glass is in the Life of Christ window (first scene, lower left) at Chartres. The window is from the twelth century.

11. In the Book of Hours, a popular devotional book from medieval times, the eight hours of the Little Office of the Blessed Virgin are introduced by a Gospel scene from the infancy of Jesus. According to the standard sequence, Matins was introduced by the Annunciation to Mary, Lauds by the Visitation, Prime by the Nativity, Terce by the annunciation to the shepherds, Sext by the adoration of the Magi, None by the Presentation in the temple, Vespers by the flight into Egypt, and Compline by the coronation of the Virgin.

    Commissioned by the wealthy, especially in the 14th and 15th centuries, manuscripts of the Book of Hours were beautifully illuminated. After the invention of printing, instead of illuminations, the Book of Hours included woodcuts or engravings of the same scenes. See Roger S. Wieck, *Painted Prayers: The Book of Hours in Medieval and Renaissance Art* (New York: George Braziller, Inc., in association with the Pierpont-Morgan Library, 1997); for the Hours of the Virgin, 51–78, for the Annunciation to Mary, 55–59. See also Janet Backhouse, *Books of Hours* (London: British Library, 1985) 15–36. For a partial facsimile of an illuminated Book of Hours, see *The Master of Mary of Burgundy: A Book of Hours for Engelbert of Nassau, The Bodleian Library, Oxford*, Introduction and Legends by J. J. G. Alexander (New York: George Braziller, 1970).

12. One of the most beautiful ivories of the Annunciation I have ever seen is in the Medieval Sculpture Hall at New York's Metropolitan Museum of Art. The Annunciation group (14th century north Italian in the international style) was lent to the museum by Father George William Rutler.

The group includes two standing figures between six and seven inches tall. The angel Gabriel (minus his wings) is depicted wearing a light cloak. By contrast, Mary is wearing ample robes, including an outer cloak and mantle.

The angel is holding a scroll, which originally must have had writing on it, most probably, *Ave, gratia plena*. Mary, somewhat taller than Gabriel, has her right hand up. In her left hand, she holds a Bible. Both figures, calmly smiling, exude a great sense of peace.

13. Andrea della Robbia (16th century) represented the Annunciation in glazed terra cotta at the Sanctuario in La Verna. In the representation, Mary has just responded, "May it be done to me according to your word." With the angel genuflecting in prayer and as the Father looks on from heaven, surrounded with cherubim, the Holy Spirit comes to Mary in the form of a dove. For a photo, see Jaroslav Pelikan, *Mary through the Centuries*, seventh illustration between pages 84 and 85.

14. Hendrick Goltzius (1558–1617) engraved "The Annunciation" (1594), in the Rijksmuseum (Amsterdam), focusing on Gabriel's response (Luke 1:30–31). In the margin below, Cornelius Schonseus translated the Latin text: "Be not afraid, girl, I am here, sent as a messenger from the kingdom of heaven on high; a virgin, you shall bear a child to the astonishment of nature, according to the predictions of the ancient Prophets, and the whole world will worship you as the mother of God" 210 (translation), 335 (the transcription of the Latin inscription). See *Hendrick Goltzius, Dutch Master (1558–1617): Drawings, Prints and Paintings*, eds., Huigen Leeflong and Ger Luijten, trans. Lynne Richards (New York: The Metropolitan Museum of Art, 2003). This catalogue was published with the exhibition in the Rijksmuseum in Amsterdam (March–May 2003), in the Metropolitan Museum of Art (June–September 2003), and in the Toledo Museum of Art in Toledo, Ohio (October 2003–January 2004).

15. See, for example, the two figures of the *Annunciation* (c. 1225–1245), standing alongside those of the *Visitation* in the west portal of the cathedral at Rheims, where a smiling Gabriel awaits Mary's response. Mary, serene and dignified, shows no anxiety. The outcome is never in doubt. For a photograph, see Michael Camille, *Gothic Art, Glorious Visions* (New York: Harry N. Abrams, 1996), 80.

16. *The Annunciation*, painted by the Flemish painter Jan van Eyck on wood (c. 1425–1430) but transferred to canvas (36 1/2 x 14 3/8"; 93 x 36.5 cm.) is in the National Gallery of Art (Andrew W. Mellon Collection) in Washington. For a reproduction, see John Walker, *National Gallery of Art, Washington*, New and Revised Edition (New York: Harry N. Abrams, Inc., 1984), 120–121, #104. As in the sculpture at Rheims, van Eyck's angel Gabriel is smiling. Mary has just accepted to be the handmaid of the Lord. She appears pensive as the Holy Spirit descends to her on a ray of light.

17. Giotto painted the Annunciation several times. Perhaps the most famous is the Scrovegni Chapel in Padua. For a photograph, see Francesca Flores d'Arcais, *Giotto*, translated by Raymond Rosenthal (New York: Abbeyville Press, 1995), 147.

18. Fra Angelico's *The Annunciation*, perhaps the most famous painting of the Annunciation, is one of the many frescoes he painted at the Dominican convent of San Marco in Florence.

19. *The Annunciation*, painted by Fra Filippo Lippi on wood (40½ x 64"; 103 x 163 cm.) shortly after 1440, is at the National Gallery of Art (Samuel H. Kress Collection), in Washington. For a reproduction, see John Walker, *National Gallery of Art, Washington*, 87 #46.

20. See *El Greco* (London: National Gallery Company Limited, 2003). El Greco (1541–1614) did many paintings of the Annunciation: *The Annunciation* in Museo Nacional del Prado (early 1570s); two paintings in Museo Thyssen-Bornemisza, Madrid (mid-1570s; c. 1597–1600, a reduced replica of the Annunciation of El Greco's large altarpiece for the Colegio de Dona Maria de Aragon in Madrid), 96–99, 104–105, 112–113, 170–171. See *El Greco of Toledo* (Boston: Little, Brown and Company, 1982), 106, for the circular painting, *The Annunciation* (c. 1603–1605) in the Hospital of Charity, which is in the town of Illescas, on the main road between Madrid and Toledo. See also *El Greco, Identity and Transformation* (Milano, Italy: Skira editore, 1999); Madrid, Central Hispano Collection (c. 1608–1622) begun by El Greco, ended by his son, Jorge Manuel, 328, 437–438.

21. See James Stevenson, *The Catacombs: Life and Death in Early Christianity* (Nashville: Thomas Nelson Publishers, 1978) 85–86; see Jaroslav Pelikan, *Mary through the Centuries*, ibid., 84–85.

22. *Ancient Christian Commentary on Scripture*, New Testament III, *Luke*, ed. Arthur A. Just Jr. (Downers Grove, Illinois: InterVarsity Press, 2003), 19–20.

23. Saint Bernard of Clairvaux (1090–1153) lived in the age of chivalry, the age of noble gentlemen, lords, knights, ladies, and vassals. In his homilies, he was among the first to call Mary "Our Lady" (*Domina Nostra*).

24. *Love without Measure: Extracts from the Writings of Saint Bernard of Clairvaux*, introduced and arranged by Paul Diemer (Kalamazoo, Michigan: Cistercian Publications, 1990), 25; Homily 4, used in the breviary office of readings for December 20 (*Hom.* 4, 8–9: *Opera omnia*, Edit. Cisterc. 4 [1966], 53–54).

25. In his *Romances* on the Gospel, *In Principio erat Verbum*, John of the Cross included two *Romances* on the Incarnation (*Romances* 7 and 8). The *Romances* were written while John of the Cross was imprisoned in Toledo (December 1577–August 1578). See Michael Dodd, OCD, "John of the Cross: The Person, His Times, His Writings," *Carmelite Studies VI: John of the Cross*, edited by Steven Payne, OCD. (Washington: Institute of Carmelite Studies, 1992), 20–21.

See also in the same volume, Emmanuel J. Sullivan, OCD, "Mary in the Writings of John of the Cross," 109–122.

For the text of *Romance 8,* see *The Collected Works of St. John of the Cross,* trans. Kieran Kavanaugh, OCD, and Otilio Rodriguez, OCD, with introductions by Kieran Kavanaugh, OCD (Washington: Institute of Carmelite Studies, 1973), 731–732.

26. John Henry Newman, *Meditations and Devotions,* with an introduction by Meriol Trevor (Burns & Oates: 1964). He died late in the evening of August 11, 1890. His meditations were first published in 1893.

27. *Lumen Gentium,* Chapter VIII, "Our Lady," V, #68. The Latin word for "image," *imago,* used by Vatican II, corresponds to the Greek word for "icon," *eikon* (see Colossians 1:15). The translation is from *Vatican Council II,* general editor, Austin Flannery, OP (Northport, N.Y.: Costello Publishing Company, Inc., 1975), 422.

28. Eager to avoid any undue Mariological emphasis, some recent exegetes and commentators stress the story's Christological message and present Mary's role as secondary. Luke's focus, however, is on Mary as a type of the church and a model for Christians, not as a privileged individual, different and set apart from all other human beings. In Luke-Acts, Christological and ecclesiological concerns are maintained in delicate balance.

29. For the term "infancy narrative," see Joseph Fitzmyer, *Luke the Theologian, Aspects of His Teaching* (New York: Paulist, 1989), 28.

30. For a discussion of the internal organization and literary structure of Luke's prologue, see Raymond E. Brown, SS, *The Birth of the Messiah,* New Updated Edition (New York: Doubleday, 1977, 1993), 248–253, 623–625.

31. For the relationship of Luke 2:41–52 to Luke 9:51–24:53, see E. LaVerdiere, *Luke,* New Testament Message 5 (Collegeville: The Liturgical Press, 1980, 1990), 37–39.

32. E. LaVerdiere, "The Original Prologue of the Gospel of Luke: Luke 3:1—4:13," *Chicago Studies,* 38/3 (Fall/Winter 1999), 249–261.

33. For a discussion concerning the relationship of the infancy narrative (1:5—2:52) to the preface (1:1–4) and what we can describe as the background and preparation for the mission and ministry of Jesus (3:1–4:13), see Fitzmyer, *Luke the Theologian,* 28–31; Brown, *The Birth of the Messiah,* 239–241, 620.

34. For a short introduction to Luke's Gospel, see Brown, *The Birth of the Messiah,* 235–239. For a much more extensive introduction, see Fitzmyer, *The Gospel According to Luke I–IX,* The Anchor Bible 28 (New York: Doubleday, 1981), 3–283. See also LaVerdiere, *Luke,* New Testament Message 5 (Collegeville: The Liturgical Press, 1980, 1990), xi–xlix.

35. In Luke's preface (1:1–4), the "eyewitnesses" and the "ministers of the word" refer to the same group, namely the disciples from the beginning of their association with Jesus. They were eyewitnesses, however, before they became ministers of the word.

36. Luke most probably wrote the two prefaces (Luke 1:1–4; Acts 1:1–2) at the same time, when he divided his "narrative of the events that have been fulfilled among us" into two volumes.

37. The beginning of the former prologue (3:1–2) corresponds to a normal beginning of a prophetic work as well as an historical work in the Hellenistic period.

38. Matthew introduced his own prologue with a genealogy, stressing a royal lineage for Jesus. In Luke, the genealogy stresses Jesus' prophetic lineage. The purpose of the genealogies is to present Jesus' identity in terms of Jesus' biblical lineage in the history of salvation. As such, Jesus' genealogy is theological and historical, much more than a biological bloodline.

39. For the story's literary form, see *Mary in the New Testament*, ed. Raymond E. Brown, Karl P. Donfried, Joseph A. Fitzmyer, and John Reumann (New York: Paulist, 1978), 111–115; Brown, *The Birth of the Messiah*, 155–159, 292–298, 629–631; Fitzmyer, *The Gospel According to Luke I–IX* (New York: Doubleday, 1981), 334–336, and *Luke the Theologian* (New York: Paulist, 1989), 46–50; E. W. Conrad, "The Annunciation of Birth and the Birth of the Messiah," *Catholic Biblical Quarterly* 47 (1985) 656–663.

40. F. O Fearghail, "Announcement or Call? Literary Form and Purpose in Luke 1:26–38," *Proceedings of the Irish Biblical Association* 16 (1993) 20–35.

41. See Robert Wilbur Neff, "The Annunciation in the Birth Narrative of Ishmael," *Biblical Research* 17 (1972) 51–60, esp. 57–59. Neff wrote a dissertation entitled *The Announcement in Old Testament Birth Stories* (Yale University, 1969), unpublished.

42. See Robert Wilbur Neff, "The Birth and Election of Isaac in the Priestly Tradition," *Biblical Research* 15 (1970) 5–18, esp. 14–16.

43. For the announcement of the birth of Ishmael, see Robert Wilbur Neff, "The Annunciation in the Birth Narrative of Ishmael," *Papers of the Chicago Society of Biblical Research* 17 (1972) 51–60.

44. The expression, "the angel of the Lord," respects the transcendence and sacredness of God while referring to God's relationship as Lord to human beings. Like other expressions, such as "the name of the Lord" or "the face of the Lord," "the angel of the Lord" is not distinct from the Lord.

45. This combination of the features is both in the biblical annunciations of birth and the biblical divine commissions to heroes: "The annunciation of Jesus' birth in Luke also involved the beginning of Mary's confrontation with the

mysterious plan of God—in other words, a type of a commissioning of Mary as the first Christian disciple." See Brown, *The Birth of the Messiah*, 629.

46. See Benjamin J. Hubbard, "Commissioning Stories in Luke-Acts: A Study of their Antecedents, Form and Content," *Semeia* 8 (1977) 103–126. The other commissioning stories include that of Balaam (Numbers 22:22–35), Joshua (Deuteronomy 31:14–15, 23; Joshua 1:1–11), Deborah (Judges 4:4–10), Samuel (1 Samuel 3:1—4:1a), Solomon (1 Chronicles 22:6–16), Elijah (1 Kings 19:1–19a), Isaiah (Isaiah 6), Jeremiah (Jeremiah 1:1–10), Ezekiel (Ezekiel 1:1—3:15), the Isaian Servant (*doulos*) of the Lord (Isaiah 49:1–6) and Cyrus (Ezra 1:1–5). For the list, see Table 1 on page 107.

# Setting and Personages

*In the sixth month, the angel*
*Gabriel was sent by God to a town (city)*
*in Galilee called Nazareth, to a virgin*
*engaged to a man whose name*
*was Joseph, of the house of David.*
*The virgin's name was Mary.*
*(Luke 1:26–27)*

The introduction of a Lukan story is very important, particularly in the prologue (1:5—2:52), where Luke's Gospel prose approaches the threshold of poetry. Reading Luke's prologue, we should remember that it was written not before but after the rest of Luke-Acts and that it represents Luke's most mature reflection on "the events that have been fulfilled among us" (1:1).

Introducing a story, Luke opens our eyes, our ears, our minds, and our hearts to see, hear, understand, and embrace the story as our own. In view of this, he selected every word, every name, every verb, every turn of phrase very carefully.

In the story of the Annunciation, the introduction presents the personages and situates the event in time and place (1:26–27). In this, Luke followed the traditional form for announcement and commissioning stories. At this point in the story, announcement and commissioning stories are quite similar.

For announcement stories, we may refer to the announcement of the birth of Isaac (Genesis 17) and the announcement of the birth of Samson (Judges 13). For the announcement of the birth of Isaac, the Lord appeared to Abram when he was ninety-nine years old (Genesis 17:1). For the announcement of the birth of Samson, an angel of the Lord appeared to the wife of a certain man from Zorah of the clan of the Danites, whose name was Manoah. Until then, Manoah's wife had been barren (Judges 13:2–3a).

For commissioning stories, we may refer to the commissioning of Moses (Exodus 3:1–4:16; 6:2–13; 7:1–6) and the commissioning of Gideon (Judges 6:11–24). In the story of the commissioning of Moses, an angel of the Lord appeared to him at Horeb, the mountain of God, while he was tending the flock of his father-in-law Jethro (Exodus 3:1–2). In the story of the commissioning of Gideon, an angel of the Lord came and sat under an oak at Ophrah belonging to Joash the Abiezrite, and appeared to his son Gideon while he was beating out wheat in the winepress, to hide it from the Midianites (Judges 6:11–12a).

In the story of the announcement of Jesus' birth and of the commissioning of Mary, the event took place in the sixth month of Elizabeth's pregnancy. That is when the angel Gabriel was sent from God to Nazareth, a city of Galilee, to a virgin named Mary, who was betrothed to a man of the house of David named Joseph (1:26–27). The introduction thus sets the stage both for the announcement of Jesus' conception and for Mary's commission to take part in the event.

## In the Sixth Month

Luke opens the story of the Annunciation by situating the event in time: "In the sixth month." That is also how he began the previous story, the annunciation to Zechariah: "In the days of Herod, King of Judea" (1:5). And that is how he would begin the next story, Mary's

Visitation to Elizabeth: "During those days" (1:39). That is how he began every story in the prologue.

As a good storyteller, Luke knew that every story begins at a certain moment in time. That is how it is with stories. That is also how it is with history, but then we call it chronology. That is also how it is when God breaks into human history, sometimes with lightning and earthshaking thunder (Exodus 19:16–19), sometimes with a tiny whisper (1 Kings 19:11–13), sometimes through the angel of the Lord, as when God spoke to Moses from a bush, aflame without being consumed (Exodus 3:1–3).

As a good storyteller, Luke also respected the ways of God entering history. The Annunciation to Mary marked a new moment in salvation history. It was "in the sixth month." The sixth month! What an extraordinary way to begin a story.

It was "in the sixth month" of Elizabeth's pregnancy with John, the one who would be called "the Baptist." At the end of the annunciation to Zechariah, "his wife Elizabeth conceived, and for five months she remained in seclusion" (1:24).[1] Now it was "in the sixth month."

It is not often that an event is dated by someone's pregnancy. But then, this was not an ordinary event. This was the announcement of the conception of Jesus, the one for whom John was conceived to prepare the way. Jesus and John were related from their very conception while being formed in their mothers' wombs before they were born (see Jeremiah 1:5).

Elizabeth was the wife of a priest named Zechariah. She and her husband were very old, "getting on in years," and until now Elizabeth had been barren (1:5–7, 18). Elizabeth and Zechariah were righteous before God, observing all the commandments and regulations of the Lord. Still, Elizabeth remained childless into her old age. In the eyes of others, Elizabeth's barrenness meant disgrace.

But Elizabeth was now pregnant. She had conceived after her husband returned from serving as priest before God (1:8–9, 23).

While Zechariah was in the sanctuary at the hour of incense offering, the angel of the Lord had appeared to him with the announcement that his wife Elizabeth would bear him a son and that he was to name him John. "Even before his birth he will be filled with the Holy Spirit" (1:15). As a prophet in "the spirit and power of Elijah," he would "make ready a people prepared for the Lord" (1:10–17).

At the end of the annunciation to Zechariah (1:5–25), we learned that "Elizabeth conceived, and for five months she remained in seclusion" (1:24), proclaiming, "This is what the Lord has done for me when he looked favorably on me and took away the disgrace I have endured among my people" (1:25). The Lord had taken away her disgrace. As a mother, she would contribute to the future of God's people. In her son, she and her husband would live beyond their years. Until now, Elizabeth had been a nobody. As a mother, she would be somebody.

The story of Zechariah and Elizabeth evokes several stories in the Old Testament, but most especially the story of Abraham and Sarah. Zechariah and Elizabeth were in their advanced years. Elizabeth was barren. An angel appeared to Zechariah, announcing the conception of a child who would play an extraordinary role in the life of God's people.

Like Zechariah, Abraham remained childless until old age. He too received an extraordinary announcement from mysterious visitors. Like Elizabeth, Sarah had been barren until, at an advanced age, she conceived a son whose name would be Isaac (Genesis 18:1–15; 21:1–8), through whom the Lord would make of Abram a great nation (12:2; 21:12).

The "sixth month" evokes the story of Zechariah and Elizabeth and with it the story of Abraham and Sarah. There is no separating the three stories. With the simple mention of "the sixth month," the three stories become one.

In the background stand Sarah and Abraham, bigger than life, and with them the entire Old Testament as a story of promise. In the mid-ground stand Elizabeth and Zechariah, epitomizing the Old Testament as a story of hope, announcing the New Testament and its story of fulfillment. In the foreground, there is Mary, the virgin, betrothed to a man named Joseph, and with her the entire New Testament with its story of fulfillment, new promise, and new hope.

Other stories also come to mind, that of the conception and birth of Ishmael (Genesis 16:7–12), for example, and another story of the conception of Isaac (17:1–21). There is also the story of the conception and birth of Samson (Judges 13:3–23). But significant as these may be, it is the story of Abraham, Sarah, and the three mysterious visitors that looms largest in the background (Genesis 18:1–15).

Set against the background of these classic stories, the story of Zechariah and Elizabeth and the conception of John is raised to epic dimensions. Like Abraham and Sarah, Zechariah and Elizabeth are bigger than life.

Evoking the story of Abraham and Sarah and other great stories, Zechariah and Elizabeth bring to mind the entire Old Testament with its old promises and ancient covenants, now seemingly barren and remembered in disgrace. But God had not forgotten his promises to Abraham. There was still life in the ancient covenant. The voice of prophecy would again be heard. Elizabeth was "in the sixth month." Soon the child would leap in her womb and be filled with the Holy Spirit at the approach of Mary pregnant with her divine child (Luke 1:39–45).

Yes, it was in the sixth month of a ten-month pregnancy,[2] the time a child shows independent life in the mother's womb. John, who would prepare the way for the Lord's coming, was quickened and received the spirit of prophecy from the very one whose way he would prepare. While the ancient covenants prepared the way for the new, they received their new life and ultimate meaning from the covenant they prepared.

# The Angel Gabriel

The angel Gabriel was sent from God to a city of Galilee named Nazareth. Six months earlier, Gabriel had appeared to Zechariah at the hour of offering incense while the whole assembly of the people was praying outside (1:8–11, 19). Like the opening expression of the story of the Annunciation to Mary, "in the sixth month," the appearance of the angel Gabriel joins the story of the Annunciation to Mary to the story of the annunciation to Zechariah, making the two events part of the same history.

Gabriel's appearance to Zechariah was no ordinary vision: "Then there appeared (*ophthe*) to him" (1:11). The Greek verb used to describe it, *ophthe*, is an aorist passive form of the verb *horao* (to see), meaning "he made himself seen."[3] In the Septuagint, this form of the verb "to see" (*ophthe*) is used exclusively for the Lord or God, the glory of God, or the angel of the Lord. For examples:

> *When Abram was ninety-nine years old, the Lord* (Kyrios) *appeared* (ophthe) *to Abram.* (*Genesis 17:1*)

> *The Lord* (*God, ho theos*) *appeared* (ophthe) *to Abraham by the oaks* (*the terebinths*) *of Mamre, as he sat in the entrance of his tent in the heat of the day.* (*Genesis 18:1*)

> *There the angel of the Lord* (aggelos kyriou) *appeared* (ophthe) *to him* (*Moses*) *in a flame of fire out of a bush.* (*Exodus 3:2*)

> *Then the glory of the Lord* (he doxa kyriou) *appeared* (ophthe) *at the tent of meeting to all the Israelites.* (*Numbers 14:10*)

The Septuagint, the Greek translation of the Hebrew Bible, was in ordinary use among the early Christians.

In the New Testament, the verb *ophthe* was part of the language of our earliest creeds (1 Corinthians 15:3b–5). It is how the Christians referred to the appearances of Jesus as risen Lord:

> *that Christ died for our sins in accordance with the scriptures; and that he was buried; and that he was raised on the third day in accordance with the scriptures; and that he appeared* (ophthe) *to Cephas, then to the Twelve. (1 Corinthians 15:3–5)*

> *Then he appeared* (ophthe) *to more than five hundred brothers and sisters at one time, most of whom are still alive, though some have died. Then he appeared* (ophthe) *to James, then to all the apostles. Last of all, as to one untimely born, he appeared* (ophthe) *also to me. (1 Corinthians 15:6–8)*

Later, Luke's Gospel used the word to announce the Lord's appearance to Simon (Peter, Cephas) when the assembled community welcomed the two disciples from Emmaus back to Jerusalem: "The Lord has risen indeed, and he has appeared (*ophthe*) to Simon" (Luke 24:34). Earlier, Luke used it to describe the appearance of Moses and Elijah at the Transfiguration of Jesus: "Suddenly they (Peter, John and James) saw two men, Moses and Elijah, talking to him. They appeared (*hoi ophthentes*) in glory and were speaking of his departure (*exodos*), which he was about to accomplish at Jerusalem" (9:30–31; see Mark 9:4).[4]

The word *ophthe,* by itself, evoked a whole world of faith, both traditional and contemporary. Gabriel's appearance to Zechariah was part of that world of faith.

The meaning of the name Gabriel in Hebrew (*gabri'el*) "El (God) is strong," or "God is my hero," speaks of divine presence and strength. We hear it in the way the angel of the Lord, standing at the right of the altar of incense, presented himself to Zechariah: "I am Gabriel. I stand in the presence of God" (Luke 1:19; see Revelation 8:2). Gabriel has a special role of messenger (1:19).

The scriptures imagined God's heavenly court in terms of an oriental court like the ancient royal court of Persia, but much better. As such, only the highest officials and functionaries were admitted into the king's presence. As one who stood before God, Gabriel joined Michael (Daniel 10:13; 12:1–3) and Raphael (Tobit 3:16–17; 5:1–12:22), and four others who "stand ready and enter before the glory of the Lord" (Tobit 12:15). The name Michael in Hebrew (*mica'el*) means "Who is like El (God)," and the name Raphael in Hebrew (*repa'el*) means "El (God) heals."

We call those seven "archangels," or leading angels. The hierarchy at the heavenly court reflected the hierarchy at oriental courts. Like Michael and Raphael, Gabriel was sent on the most sensitive missions, representing God in a very special way.[5]

The angel Gabriel came to Luke's annunciation stories with his history. Gabriel is the angel who came and stood before Daniel as a manlike figure while Daniel was pondering the meaning of a vision he had just received:

> *When I, Daniel, had seen the vision, I tried to understand it. Then someone appeared standing before me, having the appearance of a man, and I heard a human voice by the Ulai, calling "Gabriel, help this man understand the vision."*
> (*Daniel 8:15–16*)

Daniel's vision was of a ram and a powerful he-goat locked in cosmic battle (8:1–14). As Gabriel explained to Daniel, the vision was about the course of history and the end time, when an evil king, strong and powerful in his battle against the holy ones, would finally be broken by the prince of princes (8:17–26).

Gabriel is again the one who came to Daniel while Daniel was at prayer at the time of the evening sacrifice (9:20–21), the very time he came to Zechariah (Luke 1:10–11). Praying, Daniel was trying to understand Jeremiah's prophecy of the seventy years during which Jerusalem would lie in ruin (Daniel 9:1–19; see Jeremiah 11:11–12; 29:10). Gabriel gave Daniel understanding. The seventy years meant seventy weeks of years, 490 years, stretching Jeremiah's 70 years to include the time of Daniel and the desecration of the temple by the Syrian ruler Antiochus Epiphanes (Daniel 9:22–27).[6]

As God's emissary, Gabriel brought Daniel both eschatological and historical understanding, interpreting both Daniel's visions and Jeremiah's prophecy. Intimately identified with salvation history, Gabriel came to announce the time of fulfillment, when historic and cosmic fears would be finally played out and all the hopes and dreams of God's people would be realized.

Gabriel was really a great personage, an archangel, one of the seven who stand in the presence of God (see Tobit 12:15). In the Book of Revelation, "When the Lamb opened the seventh seal, there was silence in heaven for about half an hour. I saw the seven angels who stand before God, and seven trumpets were given to them" (8:1–2). In the story of the Annunciation, the mere mention of Gabriel's name brought to mind the Lord's promise and raised hopes of imminent fulfillment. The Lord had not forgotten his people.

## Was Sent by God

In the sixth month, the angel Gabriel, one who stands before God, was sent from God. The angel Gabriel was sent from God with a divine mission, to announce the conception, birth, name, and identity of Jesus as well as Mary's role in the Incarnation.

Michael was the angel of cosmic battles (Daniel 10:21–11:2; 12:1–3; Revelation 12:7–12), and Raphael the angel of divine healing (Tobit 3:16–17; 8:1–3). They too stood before God, and they too were sent on special divine missions.

Michael would be sent to guard the people of God at the time of the great distress (Daniel 8:1–3). When the prayer of Tobit and Sarah, his future daughter-in-law, "were heard in the glorious presence of God," Raphael was sent to heal Tobit's blindness and drive the demon Asmodeus from Sarah (Tobit 3:16–17).

Gabriel was the angel of the prophetic understanding, the angel of the good news. As such, Gabriel was chosen for the greatest mission of all, to announce the Incarnation. In this, Gabriel was a heavenly prototype of the elders in the Lukan churches, modeling their role as prophetic teachers, challenging, announcing, interpreting the gospel (Acts 14:23; see Luke 24:4–7).[7]

The Annunciation is part of the story of Jesus' ultimate origins in God (1:5–2:40).[8] In such a story, it stood to reason that everything of consequence would come from God, including the grace bestowed upon Mary (1:28, 30), the Holy Spirit that would overshadow her (1:35), Jesus' name (1:31; 2:21), the gospel of his birth as a savior, who would be Messiah and Lord (2:10–11), the angelic song of praise (2:13–14), and Gabriel himself with his announcement (1:26).

We should note that Gabriel was sent "from" God, not "by" God. A matter of words perhaps, but words matter. The expression "from God" (*apo tou theou*) conveys a sense of space. Being sent from God is like being sent from a place, a divine place, where God is present and an angel like Gabriel stands before him.

This sense of divine space, defined by God's presence, refers primarily to the dwelling of the Most High (1:32), Jesus' heavenly Father (2:49; 3:19–21) and the heavenly court. But it could also embrace the temple and its sanctuary, where Zechariah served before God (1:8) and, after Jesus ascended to the Father, where the community of disciples gathered and praised God continually (24:50–53; Acts 1:9–12; 2:46).

Being sent from God meant being sent from a very exalted place. That is surely significant. But to what place was Gabriel sent from God? That too must be significant.

## To a Town in Galilee Called Nazareth

In the sixth month of Elizabeth's pregnancy, the angel Gabriel, one of God's closest attendants, "was sent by (*apo*, from) God to a town in Galilee called Nazareth," literally in the original Greek, "to a city (*eis polin*) of the (*tes*) Galilee to which (the) name (*onoma*) of Nazareth." As one standing before God, Gabriel had direct access to the throne of God. He was also entrusted with the most sensitive and important missions. The contrast is striking. From his exalted position, Gabriel was sent to Nazareth, a very humble place.

Historically, Nazareth was just a town, village, or hamlet,[9] in the hills of the South of Galilee.[10] In the Gospel of John, Philip told Nathanael: "We have found him about whom Moses in the law and also the prophets wrote, Jesus son of Joseph from Nazareth." But Nathanael said to him: "Can anything good come out of Nazareth?" (John 1:45–46). Nazareth is neither mentioned in the Old Testament nor in the books of Flavius Josephus.[11] It is not mentioned in the rabbinical writings of Mishnah, Talmud, and Midrash.

Luke, however, referred to Nazareth as a city (*polis*)[12], as he did for Bethlehem (Luke 2:4), Capernaum (4:31), and other towns, suggesting the higher status conferred on them by Jesus' presence. From a civic, secular point of view, Nazareth, Bethlehem, and Capernaum were no more than little towns. But in the eyes of a Christian like Luke, they were very significant cities.[13]

It had not always been so. When the angel Gabriel was sent to announce the Incarnation, Nazareth was but a town, unknown to the vast majority of those who would be Luke's readers, living in cities such as Antioch, Ephesus, Thessalonica, Corinth, Athens, and even Rome.

Had Nazareth been a well-known place, Luke would have said more simply that the angel Gabriel was sent from God to Nazareth. Instead, he said "to a town (*eis polin*, to a city) in Galilee called Nazareth." When introducing a city that was well known to all, he was more direct. For example, referring to Jerusalem for the first time, he wrote, "When the time came for their purification according to the law of Moses, they brought him up to Jerusalem" (2:22). Referring to Antioch, he wrote, "Now those who were scattered because of the persecution that took place over Stephen traveled as far as Phoenicia, Cyprus, and Antioch" (Acts 11:19). Everybody knew about Phoenicia, Cyprus, and Antioch.[14] The same was true of Rome, first mentioned among the places represented in Jerusalem on Pentecost (1:10).

If Luke had not expected his readers to be familiar with these places, he would have referred "to a city of Judea called Jerusalem," "to a city of Syria called Antioch," and "to a city of Italy called Rome." But unlike Nazareth, these cities were well known.

There is a problem, however. At the time of Luke's writing, Nazareth was already well-known to his readers and for the very reason he called it a city; namely, because of the role Nazareth played in Jesus' life.[15] Very early on, Jesus was identified as "Jesus of Nazareth" (Mark 16:6),[16] tradition spoke of Nazareth as the place where Jesus had grown up (Luke 4:16), and outsiders identified Jesus' disciples as "the sect of the Nazarenes" (Acts 24:5).[17]

Still, Luke introduced Nazareth as "a town (city) in Galilee called Nazareth." It must be that he wanted his readers to remember the time when Nazareth was still unknown to them, thereby drawing attention to what gave Nazareth its importance. Nazareth was a humble place. It was exalted by Gabriel's mission, by Mary's openness to God's word, Jesus' conception and early years at Nazareth.

Gabriel, one who stood before the Most High, was sent to a city of Galilee called Nazareth, a lowly place that would be exalted by the name of Jesus, Son of the Most High.

## To a Virgin Engaged to a Man Whose Name Was Joseph

In the sixth month of Elizabeth's pregnancy, the angel Gabriel was sent from God to a virgin. Normally, Luke would have given the virgin's name right away, as he had just done for Nazareth, "a town (city) in Galilee called Nazareth," and was about to do for Joseph, "engaged to a man whose name was Joseph." "Whose name was Joseph," in the original Greek is literally, "to whom (the) name (*onoma*) of Joseph."

In Hebrew, Joseph is *Yosip-yah*, meaning "May the Lord (Yahweh) add." Joseph was an ancient biblical name of the patriarch Joseph:

> *Then God remembered Rachel; he heard her prayer and made her fruitful. She conceived and bore a son, and she said, "God has removed my disgrace."*[18] *So she named him Joseph, meaning, "May the Lord add another son to this one for me!"* (*Genesis 30:22–24*)

Luke was focused on the virgin, Mary. Matthew was focused on Joseph. Matthew related Joseph, the spouse of Mary (Matthew 1:19–21), to the story of the patriarch Joseph. The story of the patriarch Joseph, the son of Jacob (Israel) and Rachel (Genesis 35:22, 24), included his dreams (37:5–8, 9–10) and his being sold into Egypt (37:36). Like the patriarch Joseph, the story of Joseph, the son of David, featured his dreams (Matthew 1:20–21; 2:13, 19–20) and the flight to Egypt (2:13–15).

But in this case, Luke withheld the name, identifying Mary simply as "a virgin," in Greek *parthenos*, a virgin who was "engaged (betrothed) to a man whose name was Joseph," who was "of the house of David." Only after that did he give the name of the virgin: "The virgin's name was Mary." Clearly, Luke wanted to emphasize that the angel Gabriel was sent from God to a virgin.

It is very significant that the angel Gabriel was sent "to a virgin." There is a tendency today to take the word lightly and even dismiss it here as a reference simply to a young woman. In support of this, some refer to the well-known passage from Isaiah: "Look (*idou*, behold), the young woman (*he parthenos*, the virgin) is with child and shall bear a son, and shall name him Immanuel (*Emmanouel*)" (Isaiah 7:14).

In Isaiah 7:14, the Hebrew word translated as "virgin" is *'alma*, a term whose meaning is broader than the English word, "virgin." The Hebrew word *'alma* can refer to a virgin, but its general meaning is "young woman." The Septuagint's Greek translation of *'alma* is *parthenos*, the very word found in Luke's Annunciation to Mary, "to a virgin (*parthenos*) engaged to a man whose name was Joseph" (1:27).

Isaiah 7:14 referred to the mother of king Hezekiah before she conceived the future king. At the time and until she conceived, Hezekiah's mother was a virgin. But when she became with child and bore a son, she was no longer a virgin.

The meaning of the Hebrew term *'alma* in Isaiah 7:14 and its translation into Greek as *parthenos* may be of interest in a study of Matthew 1:18–25, which refers to Isaiah 7:14 and actually quotes the text (Matthew 1:23), but not in a study of Luke 1:26–27. Unlike Matthew, Luke does not refer to Isaiah 7:14. Nor does he show any interest in the Hebrew terms underlying their Greek translation whether in the Septuagint or in early Christian usage.

The expression Luke used in 1:27, "to a virgin engaged to a man" (*pros parthenon emnesteumenen andri*) is a clear reference to Deuteronomy 22:23, which introduces the laws governing "a young girl (*pais*) who is a virgin betrothed to a man" (*pais parthenos memnesteumene andri*). In the text from Deuteronomy, the term *parthenos* further specifies the term *pais* (young girl).

A young girl (*pais*) might or might not be a virgin (*parthenos*). The two terms were not equivalent. Deuteronomy 22:23 refers to someone who is both a "young girl" and a "virgin." The latter term, *parthenos*, implies that the young girl was of marriageable age. The laws for a young girl who is a virgin and who is engaged (betrothed) are then given in Deuteronomy 22:23–27. Following these is a law governing "a virgin who is not engaged" (*ten paida* [the young girl] *ten parthenon* [the virgin], *hetis ou memnesteutai*) (22:28–29).

Legal texts such as these, which are part of the laws governing sexual relations (22:13–30), are extremely important because of their careful use of terminology. We learn from them that *aner*, which means "man" in the sense of "husband," also refers to a man to whom a woman is engaged (betrothed).[19] We also learn that the term *gyne*, meaning "woman" in the sense of "wife," also refers to a woman who is engaged (betrothed) but is still a virgin (22:24) as well as to a woman who has had sexual relations with a man and is no longer a virgin (22:29).

The term *aner* is applied to Joseph in Luke 1:27. On the other hand, Luke avoids the term *gyne* in reference to Mary. Even later, in the story of Jesus' birth, Luke refers to her as Joseph's engaged (betrothed, *emnesteumene*, 2:5). The story may have not called for a reference to Mary as *gyne*. It may also be that Luke wanted to avoid any ambiguity. Later, Elizabeth greets her relative as "the mother of my Lord" (1:43).

After Jesus' birth, Luke refers to Mary as "his mother" (*he meter autou*, 2:33, 34, 48, 51). Since there was no longer any ambiguity about Jesus' origins, Luke also refers to Joseph as "his father" (*ho pater autou*, 2:33, 48). Together, Mary and Joseph were Jesus' parents (*hoi goneis autou*, 2:41).

In a parallel story, Matthew refers to Joseph as Mary's husband (*aner*, Matthew 1:19; see also 1:16) and to Mary as Joseph's wife (*gyne*, 1:20, 24), but only while Mary is pregnant with Jesus. At the same time, Matthew stresses that Mary is still a virgin. After the birth of Jesus, he always refers to Mary as the mother (*meter*) of the child (*paidion*, 1:18; 2:11, 13, 14; 2:20, 21), never as the wife (*gyne*) of

Joseph. In their way, both Luke and Matthew emphasize that Mary, the mother of Jesus, was a virgin.

Consequently, there is no reason to question the meaning of the term *parthenos* as used in 1:27. It clearly means "virgin," in the sense of a woman who has never had sexual relations with a man. As we shall see, Luke's story of the Annunciation depends on the virginity of Mary. Without Mary's virginity, the whole story would collapse.

Describing a young woman as a virgin says that she has not had sexual relations with a man. In a traditional culture, this was very important in relation to a possible future marriage. Describing her as a virgin, not having had sexual relations, also says that she was not a mother. In relation to a woman's status among the Jewish people, that was even more important.

Mary may have been "engaged (betrothed) to a man whose name was Joseph," but he had not yet taken her to live with him in his home, and she was not a mother. In the Jewish society of the time as well as in Roman society, the purpose of marriage was to have children.[20] Since Mary was still a virgin and had no child, she and Joseph had not yet fulfilled the purpose of their betrothal and marriage.

To be really somebody in a traditional culture, including that of the Jews in New Testament times, a woman had to be a mother. That is how a woman contributed to building up the people of God, her own people, ensuring at the same time that she and her husband would live into the next generation and hopefully into the generation after that. To be a truly great person, a woman had to have many children, ensuring a great future for her, her husband, her family, indeed, for the people of God.

In that context, being a virgin meant being just a virgin. Being a childless woman like Elizabeth meant being excluded from the blessing God granted Adam and Eve:

*So God created humankind in his image, in the image of God*
*he created them; male and female he created them. God blessed*
*them, and God said to them, "Be fruitful and multiply, and fill*
*the earth and subdue it; and have dominion over the fish of the*
*sea and over the birds of the air and over every living thing that*
*moves upon the earth." (Genesis 1:27–28)*

In relation to a young girl who was a virgin, sharing in that blessing
remained a possibility but was not yet fulfilled. Until it was fulfilled,
when a virgin becomes a mother, a young girl remained a person of
little consequence.

Gabriel, an angel of great stature in the heavenly court, came
to a virgin, a woman of lowly stature in the eyes of human society.
Today, as we look back on two thousand years of Christianity, we
celebrate a history rich with heroic Christians, many of whom were
virgins. Consider, for example, Saint Scholastica, Saint Clare, Saint
Teresa of Avila, Saint Catherine of Siena, and Saint Thérèse of
Lisieux. Because of them and many others, a consecrated virgin,
dedicated to God and the mission of Christ, is honored as a person
of great stature, witnessing to the mission of Christ.

It was not so in New Testament times, when a virgin was a
lowly person. We need to remember that in relation to Mary. Our
tendency is to see Mary as one exalted from the start and forget
that the angel Gabriel was sent from God to exalt the lowly.
As Mary sings in her Magnificat:[21]

*My soul magnifies the Lord,*
    *and my spirit rejoices in God my Savior,*
*for he has looked with favor on the lowliness of his servant.*
    *Surely, from now on all generations will call me blessed.*
*(Luke 1:46–48)*

# Of the House of David

"The angel Gabriel was sent by (*apo*) God . . . to a virgin engaged (betrothed) to a man whose name was Joseph, of the house of David." As a virgin, the young woman may have been lowly, but she was engaged to a man who was of the house of David. Many surely could claim the same. The house of David counted a very large number of descendants after more than 900 years. Normally, being of the house of David would not have been very significant and would not have been mentioned.

Luke, however, did indicate that the virgin's husband, Joseph, was of the house of David. Therefore, in Joseph's case, it must have been significant. In the story of Jesus' birth, Luke again associated Joseph with the house of David: "Joseph also went from the town (*polis*) of Nazareth in Galilee to Judea, to the city (*polis*) of David called Bethlehem, because he was descended from the house and family of David. He went to be registered with Mary, to whom he was engaged and who was expecting a child" (2:4–5). Later, in Jesus' genealogy (3:23–38), Luke presented Joseph (3:23) as descended from David (3:31).

A long history of messianic hope looked to the family of David for a Messiah. In his canticle, Zechariah referred to that history:

> He has raised up a mighty savior for us (*Greek: a horn for our salvation*)
>> in the house of his servant David,
>> as he spoke through the mouth of his holy prophets
>>> from of old,
> that we would be saved from our enemies
> and from the hand of all who hate us.
> (*Luke 1:69–71*)

Jesus "was the son (as was thought) of Joseph son of Heli" (Luke 3:23). Through Joseph, Jesus was related to the house of David, as Zechariah sang in his canticle. While being of the house of David, Jesus also transcended the house of David, as Jesus himself would show toward the end of his life while teaching in the temple:

> Then [Jesus] said to [the Sadducees],
> "How can they say that the Messiah is David's Son?
> For David himself says in the book of Psalms,
> > 'The Lord said to my Lord,
> > > "Sit at my right hand
> > > > until I make your enemies your footstool."'
> David thus calls him Lord; so how can he be his son?"
> (Luke 20:41–44)

While raised up "in the house of his servant David" (1:69), Jesus transcended the house of David. Our earliest Christian witness to this tradition is a little creed Paul quoted in his letter to the Romans. Paul was set apart for the gospel of God, the gospel of his Son, "who was descended from David according to the flesh, but was declared to be Son of God with power according to the spirit of holiness by resurrection from the dead, Jesus Christ our Lord" (Romans 1:3–4).[22] According to the Acts, Paul preached in the synagogue of Antioch in Pisidia:

> When he had removed him, he made David their king. In his testimony about him he said, "I have found David, son of Jesse, to be a man after my heart, who will carry out all my wishes." Of this man's posterity God has brought to Israel a Savior, Jesus, as he promised. (Acts 13:22–23)

# The Virgin's Name was Mary

The introduction now comes to an end. To this point, Luke referred to Mary as "a virgin engaged to a man whose name was Joseph, of the house of David." Nazareth had just been introduced as "a town (*polis*, city) in Galilee," and Joseph is introduced as "a man whose name was Joseph." Had Luke followed the same pattern, he would have written, "In the sixth month the angel Gabriel was sent by God to a town in Galilee called Nazareth, to a virgin *whose name was Mary*, engaged to a man *whose name was Joseph*, of the house of David." By breaking the pattern, Luke highlighted Mary's virginity and her singular role in the story.

It is only at the very end of the introduction that Luke gives Mary's name: "The virgin's name was Mary."[23] Introducing a virgin and then identifying her as a virgin whose name was Mary, Luke seems to presuppose that Mary was unknown to his readers. It is as though he had to introduce her for the very first time, as he did for Nazareth, "a town (city) in Galilee," and Joseph, "a man . . . of the house of David." He did not have to do that for the angel Gabriel, whom he introduced directly, "the angel Gabriel," not "an angel whose name was Gabriel."

Luke uses a brief statement presenting Mary's name: "The virgin's name was Mary." For Luke, it is important that Mary is a virgin (*parthenos*). In the context of the Gospel, this places her in a category by herself; the term is never again used in Luke's Gospel. In the Annunciation to Mary (1:26–38), "the virgin" has a significant value for Christology.

Mary the virgin would give birth to a holy child who would be called Son of God (1:35b). Such a child could not be conceived in the ordinary way by sexual relations with a man. The child could be conceived only by the Holy Spirit (1:35a). In so conceiving, Mary remained a virgin. Mary's virginity thus transcends that of ordinary virgins.

For Luke, Mary's name is also important: "The virgin's name was Mary."[24] Luke shows that he found great significance in a person's name, including Zechariah and Elizabeth (1:5), Joseph and Mary (1:27), John, son of Zechariah (1:60, 63; 3:2) Simeon (2:25), Anna (2:36), Simon Peter (5:8), James and John, sons of Zebedee (5:10), Levi (5:27), Mary, called Magdalene (8:2), Joanna and Susanna (8:3), and so on.

In this, Luke was not unique. In the ancient cultures reflected in the Bible, a name revealed the person's mysterious identity and gave a certain claim to that person's attention. That is why the various works in the Old and New Testaments avoid giving God a name. God revealed the divine name to Moses, "I AM WHO I AM" (Exodus 3:14).[25] I AM was presence to his people. The "name" (*to onoma*) of God was frequently used as a substitute for Yahweh (*kyrios*, Lord).

It is possible, however, to refer to God's name as Mary does in the Magnificat, "holy is his name" (1:49), and as every Christian does in the Lord's Prayer, "Father, hallowed be your name" (11:2). Both of these texts help us grasp the implications of Luke's "the virgin's name was Mary" somewhat better.

In the Magnificat, we should note whose name is said to be holy. To say God is too simple. In the immediate context of Luke 1:49, the one whose name is holy is "the Mighty One." In the more general context, it is the Lord and God who is Mary's Savior (1:47).

In the Lord's Prayer, the name, like the kingdom, does not refer to God but to the Father. It is true, of course, that the Father is God, but the prayer approaches God from a particular point of view and a special relationship to those who pray this prayer. The name to be hallowed is the source of our life, the one to whom we are indebted at every moment for both human life, which comes to us from birth, and life in the Spirit, which comes to us from Baptism.

In the story of the Annunciation, the name does not refer to a young girl or maiden. Nor does it refer to a person in general. It is the name of the virgin to whom the angel Gabriel had been sent by God. Luke thus means to highlight Mary's identity precisely as a virgin, as the one who conceived the Son of the Most High through the power of the Holy Spirit. The name is meant to communicate Mary's person as fully open to God's life and creativity: "Here am I, the servant of the Lord; let it be with me according to your word" (1:38).

Up to this point in these reflections, we have tried to acquire a keener sense of Luke's reference to Mary as a virgin and of his approach to her identity. What can we say about the name Mary, the personal name of the virgin who conceived by the Holy Spirit the Son of God?

Like the name Joseph, which evokes the patriarchal Joseph, the name Mary is an ancient biblical name, especially of Miriam (in Hebrew, *Miryam*), the sister of Moses and Aaron (LXX, Exodus 6:20;[26] Numbers 26:59)[27] and prophetess:

> *Then the prophet Miriam, Aaron's sister, took a tambourine in her hand; and all the women went out after her with tambourines and with dancing. And Miriam sang to them:*
> *"Sing to the Lord, for he has triumphed gloriously; horse and rider he has thrown into the sea." (Exodus 15:20–21)*

In the Old Testament, only one woman, the sister of Moses and Aaron, is named Miriam (Mary; LXX, *Mariam*). In the New Testament, seven women are named Mary (in Greek, *Mariam* or *Maria*), including:

1. Mary "the mother of Jesus" (Acts 1:14), and the mother of "the Son of the Most High" (Luke 1:32) and the "Son of God" (Luke 1:35);

2. Mary "called Magdalene" (Luke 8:2; John 19:25) from the town of Magdala on the western shore of the Sea of Galilee;[28]

3. Mary "the mother of James" (Luke 24:10);

4. Mary the sister of Martha (John 11:1; see Luke 10:38–42);[29]

5. Mary "the mother of John whose other name was Mark" (Acts 12:12);

6. Mary, a member of the church at Rome, "who has worked very hard among you" (Romans 16:6); and

7. Mary "the wife of Clopas" (John 19:25).

Of course, everyone, that is, all of Luke's readers, already knew Mary. Mark had referred to her by name in his Gospel: "Is not this the carpenter, the son of Mary (*ho huios tes Marias*) . . . ?" (Mark 6:3). Mary was a member of the early community of disciples in Jerusalem, even before the Holy Spirit came on Pentecost: "All these were constantly devoting themselves to prayer, together with certain women, including Mary the mother of Jesus, as well as his brothers" (Acts 1:14).[30]

As in the case of Nazareth, it must be that Luke wanted his readers to remember a time when Mary was still unknown and just a lowly virgin, not yet a mother. In that way, all would recognize why Mary, the lowly virgin, was exalted, indeed, blessed beyond all women (Luke 1:42).

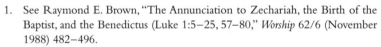

1. See Raymond E. Brown, "The Annunciation to Zechariah, the Birth of the Baptist, and the Benedictus (Luke 1:5–25, 57–80," *Worship* 62/6 (November 1988) 482–496.

2. See Wisdom 7:2, where the term of a pregnancy is described as ten months. The same is presupposed in Luke's prologue. Mary goes to visit Elizabeth when her relative is "in the sixth month" (1:26), remains with her "about three months" (1:56) and returns home before Elizabeth gives birth to John (1:57). As he would do at Jesus' baptism, Luke wishes to show that, while Jesus was related to John, his mission represented an entirely new divine intervention.

3. See E. LaVerdiere, "Before Ever There Was a Name," *Emmanuel* 100 (Jan./Feb., 1994) 7; *The Eucharist in the New Testament and the Early Church* (Collegeville: The Liturgical Press, 1996), 4–5.

4. In the Acts of the Apostles, *ophthe* and various related forms are used quite often, beginning at Pentecost with the appearance of tongues as of fire (Acts 2:3), four times in Stephen's discourse (7:2, 26, 30, 35), after that for various appearances to Paul (9:17; 16:9; 26:16), and once in a discourse of Paul (13:31).

5. All three play an important role in the Book of Enoch, where Michael is the most prominent (Enoch 9:1; 10:11; passim). For Raphael, see Enoch 10:4 and 40:9. For Gabriel, see Enoch 9:1, 20:7, and 40:9.

6. Antiochus IV Epiphanes (175–164 BC) was responsible for a great persecution of the Jewish people (167–164). In 167, he established the cult of Olympian Zeus in the temple at Jerusalem (see Daniel 8:11–12; 11:31; 1 Maccabees 1:41–63; 2 Maccabees 6:1–11). The expression in Daniel 11:31; 12:11; 1 Maccabees 1:54, "the desolating abomination," very likely refers to the new cult.

7. The seventy or seventy-two whom Jesus appointed (Luke 10:1–12) for the journey to Jerusalem and the Ascension (9:51) recall the seventy elders of Israel chosen to assist Moses in the Exodus as prophetic teachers (Numbers 11:16–30). Jesus sent the seventy[-two] "in pairs to every town and place where he himself intended to go" (Luke 10:1; see 9:52–55). The two men who speak to the women in the tomb are one of those pairs. They model the role of Christian elders as prophetic teachers in the Lukan churches.

8. E. LaVerdiere, *Luke*, New Testament Message 5 (Collegeville: The Liturgical Press, 1980, 1990), 9–13.

9. Joseph Fitzmyer describes Nazareth as "this insignificant Galilean hamlet," *The Gospel According to Luke I–IX*, The Anchor Bible 28 (New York: Doubleday, 1981), 343, note 1:26. Michael Patella, OSB, describes Nazareth in "Seers' Corner: Nazareth," *The Bible Today* 41/2 (March/April 2003) 103: "What was a small, obscure, and forgotten village over two thousand years ago has become one of the most well-known places of the Christian world today."

10. See Sean Freyne, "Galilee (Hellenistic/Roman)," *The Anchor Bible Dictionary* (New York: Doubleday, 1992), 2:895–899; Josephus, *The Jewish War*, The Loeb Classical Library (Cambridge: Harvard University Press, 1967), Book II: 188–191, 2:396–397; Book III: 35–40, 2:584–587.

11. Flavius Josephus (AD 37–*circa* 100) wrote four books: (1) *Life of Josephus* (autobiography), (2) *The Jewish War* (AD 66–73, the first war), (3) *The Jewish Antiquities*, and (4) *Against Apion*.

12. Luke referred to Nazareth as a city three times, 1:26; 2:4, 39.

13. It may also be that Luke wanted to adapt the Gospel story to the context of his readers, most of whom lived in cities.

14. See also Acts 6:5, where Luke refers to "Nicholas of Antioch, a convert from Judaism."

15. Nazareth is mentioned in relation to Jesus' life, first in Mark 1:9 and then in Luke 1:26; 2:4, 39, 51; 4:16. Jesus is referred to as "Jesus of Nazareth" (*Iesous ton apo Nazareth*) in Acts 10:38.

16. Since Jesus came from Nazareth, he was identified first as "Jesus the Nazarene" (*Iesous ho Nazarenos*) in Mark 10:47; 14:67; 16:6; and Luke 4:34; 24:19. Using the vocative, an unclean spirit addresses him simply as "Jesus Nazarene" (*Iesou Nazarene*) without the definite article (Mark 1:24). In Luke-Acts, the title is usually "Jesus Christ the Nazorean" (*Iesous Christos ho Nazoraios*, Acts 3:6; 4:10) or "Jesus the Nazorean" (Luke 18:37; Acts 2:22; 6:14; 22:8; 26:9).

17. Because of their association with "Jesus the Nazorean" (see the previous note), the followers of Jesus came to be described as "the sect of the Nazoreans."

18. Like Rachel, Elizabeth said: "This is what the Lord has done for me when he looked favorably on me and took away the disgrace I have endured among my people" (Luke 1:25).

19. For the legal age of the marriage and betrothal, "The legal minimum age of marriage was 12 for girls and 14 for boys, and betrothal could take place some time before that: Augustus fixed the minimum age for betrothal at 10. . . . It is worth noting, however, that Augustus' laws did not begin to penalize young people for non-marriage until a girl was 20 and a man 25." See Beryl Rawson, "The Roman Family," in *The Family in Ancient Rome, New Perspectives*, ed. Beryl Rawson (Ithaca: Cornell University Press, 1986), 21–22.

20. See Beryl Rawson, "The Roman Family," *The Family in Ancient Rome, New Perspectives*, ed. Beryl Rawson (Ithaca: Cornell University Press, 1986), 1–57, see esp. 8–15.

21. See Robert J. Karris, OFM, "Mary's Magnificat," *The Bible Today* 39/3 (May/June 2001) 145–149; Raymond E. Brown, SS, *The Birth of the Messiah*, (New York: Doubleday, 1993), 336–338, 346–365, 642–655.

22. See Joseph A. Fitzmyer, *Romans*, The Anchor Bible 33 (New York: Doubleday, 1993), 229–230, 233–237; *Mary in the New Testament*, edited by Raymond E. Brown, Karl P. Donfried, Joseph A. Fitzmyer, and John Reumann (New York: Paulist, 1978), 34–40; Simon Legasse, "Fils de David et Fils de Dieu, Note sur Romains 1,3–4," *Nouvelle Revue Theologique* 122/4 (Octobre-Decembre 2000) 564–572.

23. The name "Mary" is known from the Old Testament as the name of Moses' sister, "Miriam," in Hebrew *Miryam* (Exodus 15:20), which the Septuagint translated as *Mariam*, the Greek form Luke used in 1:27. Mary was a popular name in Hellenistic Judaism.

24. As Joseph Fitzmyer points out in his notes on this verse, the name Mary is from *Miryam*, a Semitic name of ancient Canaanite origin, which is related to

the word meaning "height, summit"; as the name of Mary evokes the idea of "Excellence" (*The Gospel According to Luke I–IX,* The Anchor Bible 28 [New York: Doubleday, 1981], 344). Besides "Excellence," I would like to suggest "Exalted," an etymology associated with the entire Magnificat, which celebrates the exaltation of the lowly.

25. In the Septuagint, God's name is *ego eimi ho on,* which translated into English is, "I am the one who is."

26. In the Septuagint, Exodus 6:20 differs from the original Hebrew. "And Ambram took to wife Jochabed the daughter of his father's brother, and she bore to him both Aaron and Moses and Mariam (*Mariam*) their sister" (LXX); "Amran married Jochabed his father's sister and she bore him Aaron and Moses" (Hebrew). See John William Wevers, *LXX, Notes on the Greek Text of Exodus,* Number 30 (Atlanta: Scholars Press, 1990), 84–85.

27. See Exodus 6:20 (LXX); 15:20, 21; Numbers 12:1, 4, 5, 10 (twice), 15 (twice); 20:1; 26:59; Deuteronomy 24:9; 1 Chronicles 5:29 (LXX), 6:3 (Hebrew); and Micah 6:4.

28. See James F. Strange, "Magdala," *The Anchor Bible Dictionary* (New York: Doubleday, 1992), 4:463–464.

29. See E. LaVerdiere, *Dining in the Kingdom of God* (Chicago: Liturgy Training Publications, 1994), 75–86.

30. Mary, the mother of Jesus, is mentioned by name in Mark 6:3; Matthew 1:16, 18, 20; 2:11; 13:55; Luke 1:27, 30, 34, 38, 39, 41, 46, 56; 2:5, 16, 19, 34; Acts 1:14.

# The Angel's Greeting to Mary and Mary's Reaction

*And he came to her and said,*
*"Greetings, favored one*
*(Chaire, kecharitomene)!*
*The Lord is with you*
*(ho kyrios meta sou)."*
*But she was much perplexed*
*by his words (epi to logo)*
*and pondered what sort of greeting*
*this might be.*
*(Luke 1:28–29)*

Introducing the story of the Annunciation, Luke presented its two personages, the angel Gabriel and a virgin whose name was Mary. He also set the event in time and place. It was "in the sixth month" that "the angel Gabriel was sent by God to a town (to a city, *eis polin*) of Galilee called Nazareth, to a virgin engaged to a man whose name was Joseph, of the house of David" (1:26–27).

The introduction, "Setting and Personages" (1:26–27), also sets the Annunciation to Mary (1:26–38) against the background of the annunciation to Zechariah (1:5–25). Six months before, Gabriel had appeared to Zechariah in the sanctuary of the Lord, while Zechariah was about to offer incense at the afternoon hour of prayer. Appearing to Zechariah, Gabriel announced that his wife

Elizabeth would bear him a son whom he was to name John. Their son would be great in the sight of the Lord. He would prepare a people fit for the Lord (1:5–25).

Now, in the sixth month of Elizabeth's pregnancy, Gabriel was sent from God to a city of Galilee called Nazareth to a virgin whom name was Mary. In her old age,[1] Elizabeth had conceived, and she was in her sixth month. We expect the angel to announce that Mary, the young virgin, would also conceive. The annunciation to Zechariah prepared the Annunciation to Mary, just as John the Baptist, the forerunner, would prepare the way of the Lord (1:17, 76; 3:4–6).

Why was Gabriel sent from God to Mary? Gabriel had appeared to Zechariah, the father of the child, but not to his mother Elizabeth. Why was Gabriel not sent to Joseph?[2] The two stories of annunciation would be very different. As the father of John, Zechariah had a major role in the story of John's conception. Joseph has no role at all in the story of the conception of Jesus.

After introducing the story (1:26–27), Luke opens the dialogue between the angel Gabriel and the virgin Mary. We expect something extraordinary. Nothing, however, has prepared us for the angel's greeting to Mary.

As we have seen, the dialogue unfolds in three phases:

1. the angel's greeting to Mary and Mary's reaction (1:28–29);

2. the angel's announcement to Mary and Mary's question (1:30–34);

3. the angel's answer to Mary's question and Mary's response (1:35–38a).

We now enter the first phase (1:28–29), where Gabriel comes to Mary and greets her (1:28), and Mary reacts to Gabriel's word of greeting, but not verbally. Deeply troubled, Mary ponders what the greeting means (1:29). We may view this first phase of the dialogue as introductory.

Some of the most meaningful greetings are without words. The greeting may be conveyed with a warm smile, a tearful embrace, a sincere handshake, a welcoming nod, or a respectful bow. Much depends on the culture, the situation, and the relationship between the people involved.

I remember watching members of a Vietnamese family arriving at an airport in the Midwest, being greeted by the rest of the family after many years of separation. They were just arriving from Vietnam, a long trip. The women wore traditional garb. The men had smart new suits. I shall never forget the moment they caught sight of one another through a glass wall, clutching at the glass, straining to get through. I shall never forget the grandparents seeing their little grandchild for the first time, silently and gently cradling the child in their arms, and the little children in awe before grandparents they had known only in photographs. Not a word was spoken. They simply embraced, over and over again. And they cried.

That was a greeting! No question that it was meaningful. I am referring to the greeting itself as an event, something much greater than words. In this case, there were no words.

Most of the time, a greeting is spoken in words, but the words used and their significance are secondary. Their function is to acknowledge and recognize someone, or to convey the emotional excitement and the joy of meeting. For that, even a simple "Hi!" or "Hello!" is adequate, given that the greeting is expressed in a person's attitude, tone of voice, pitch, and intonation, the language of the voice, the face, and the body. There is more to a greeting than words. The same words, "hi" or "hello," can be spoken perfunctorily, when someone wants to be civil, but no more.

In the scriptures, greetings are always very meaningful, even if the greeting is unspoken. For example, consider the father's greeting in the story of the prodigal son. Seeing his son from a distance, the father ran to greet him. Saying nothing, he embraced his son and kissed him. His son had returned (see Luke 15:20). The son had prepared a little speech for his father: He was no longer worthy to be his son, he should be treated as one of his father's hired hands. From the father's greeting, we knew that the son's prepared speech would be ignored.

The words, of course, make a difference. They spell out the meaning of the encounter, the relationship, or the event. For that, we have many examples in the New Testament, including Gabriel's greeting to Mary, where the encounter gives meaning to the words, which in turn spell out the meaning of the event. We would not understand the meaning of the greeting, "Greetings (hail), favored (fully graced) one!" without the angel's announcement. Nor would we understand Mary's role in the Incarnation without the angel's greeting, "Greetings (hail), favored (fully graced) one!"

Jesus' greeting to Mary Magdalene also comes to mind. Mary was grieving Jesus' death. Risen from the dead, he greeted her by name, "Mary!" At that, she recognized him, "Rabbouni"[3] (John 20:16). In that case, the greeting was Mary Magdalene's very name. We also remember the distinctive greeting of the risen Lord to the disciples, "Peace be with you" (Luke 24:36; John 20:19, 21, 26).

Sometimes, the words are extremely significant. Consider also the greeting in the prayer the Lord Jesus taught his disciples, "Father," (Luke 11:2), "Our Father in heaven" (Matthew 5:9). When we greet God as "Father," or "Our Father," we acknowledge that God is the source of our life, not only as human beings but as Christians, transformed by grace. The greeting also acknowledges that as Christians, brothers and sisters in Christ, we are sons and daughters of God (Romans 8:14–17; Galatians 3:26–28).

Consider also Paul's greeting to the church at Thessalonica, "Grace (*charis*) to you and peace (1 Thessalonians 1:1), or its more developed form, "Grace (*charis*) to you and peace from God our Father and the Lord Jesus Christ" (1 Corinthians 1:3). As we shall see, the ordinary Greeks and Romans greeted one another in Greek with *chaire* (hail!) or *chairein* (greetings!), and the ordinary Jews greeted one another in Hebrew with *shalom* (peace!).

Paul greeted the churches and individual Christians with *charis* (grace!), which is distinctly Christian. Grace is God's gift offered through Jesus Christ. The term *charis* may have been chosen by reason of its assonance with *chairein*, but it represents a far more important biblical concept that is here applied in a Christian context.

It is in this light that we have to consider Gabriel's greeting to Mary: "Greetings" (*chaire*, hail), favored one (*kecharitomene*)." In the story of the Annunciation, the angel Gabriel was sent from God to a virgin named Mary with a momentous mission. That mission called for a very meaningful greeting.

At this point, we should remember that there is more to a greeting than the words we speak. How can we convey Gabriel's attitude and tone of voice? Somehow we have to do it through our own attitude and tone of voice. Luke did it through Greek. We have to do it through English or some other modern language.

Gabriel's words had to be carefully chosen and significant: "Greetings (*chaire*, hail), favored one (*kecharitomene*, fully graced)! The Lord is with you (*ho kyrios meta sou*)." For all its simplicity, Gabriel's greeting is full of mystery. It is also full of faith and theology.

How then can we render a greeting that is so rich in divine presence, mystery and theology? How, for that matter, can we render any greeting in the New Testament, for example, Elizabeth's greeting in the following story: "Blessed are you among women, and blessed is the fruit of your womb" (Luke 1:42), or the Lord's greeting to the assembled community in Jerusalem: "Peace be with you" (24:36)?[4]

Behind the Lord's "peace" stands a great Hebrew greeting, *shalom*, in the Greek of the New Testament, *eirene*. In the Old Testament, *shalom* summed up the blessings of God's covenant with a chosen people. In the New Testament, *eirene* summed up the blessings of the new covenant of grace, uniting all peoples into one people of God. It is the Lord Jesus, the one who died for our sins and was raised from the dead (see 1 Corinthians 15:3–5), who greets the disciples with "Peace!" It is very hard to render such a greeting. It is also hard to render the angel's greeting to Mary, "*Chaire, kecharitomene!*"

## And He Came to Her and Said

The angel Gabriel was sent from God to a virgin betrothed to a man named Joseph. "Coming to her," the angel now fulfilled his mission. Sent from God, the angel Gabriel came to Mary. It all happened in an instant.

Journeys are an important theme in Luke-Acts.[5] Here in the prologue, we have Mary's journey to her relative, Elizabeth (Luke 1:39–56), the journey of Joseph and Mary to Bethlehem and Jerusalem (2:1–40) and the journey of Jesus and his parents to Jerusalem (2:41–52). Such journeys took time. Gabriel's journey, from his exalted position before God to the lowly virgin of Nazareth, did not. The distance from God to us is not measured in miles or kilometers.

The angel Gabriel was sent in the sixth month of Elizabeth's pregnancy. Earlier, Gabriel appeared to Zechariah (1:11). He had been sent to Zechariah with good news (1:19). Zechariah's prayer had been heard. His wife Elizabeth would bear him a son, whom he would name John. He and Elizabeth would have joy and gladness and many would rejoice at his birth. Their son would be great in the sight of the Lord (1:13–14). Now, when the angel Gabriel was sent to Mary, Elizabeth was in her sixth month.

But something even more extraordinary was about to be fulfilled in our midst (1:1). Mary, the virgin, would conceive in her womb and bear a son, whom she would name Jesus (1:31). For this, God would need Mary's cooperation, her *fiat*. Gabriel came to Mary to announce the conception and birth of Jesus. At the same time, Gabriel came with a commission for the virgin Mary. Together, the announcement and the commission constitute two inseparable aspects of what we call "the Annunciation."

The Annunciation begins with a greeting never before heard, one to which Mary reacted with consternation and wonderment. In terms of the literary form, the greeting connects the Annunciation with the traditional form for commission stories, where the focus is on the person who receives the commission.

In the biblical stories announcing a birth, the focus is on the child to be born, not on his mother or father. Accordingly, in the stories announcing the birth of Isaac (Genesis 17), Samson (Judges 13), John the Baptist (Luke 1:5–25) and Jesus (Luke 2:8–14), God, the angel of the Lord, and Gabriel do not greet Abraham, the wife of Manoah, Zechariah, and the shepherds of Bethlehem; they simply appear.

In the stories of commission, the angel of the Lord or the Lord greets by name, "Moses, Moses!" (Exodus 3:4), "Do not be afraid, Abram" (Genesis 15:1), "Jacob, Jacob" (Genesis 46:2), "Samuel! Samuel!" (1 Samuel 3:10), "Joseph, son of David" (Matthew 1:20), and "Saul, Saul" (Acts 9:4).

## "Greetings, Favored One! (*Chaire, kecharitomene*)"

Gabriel's greeting to Mary, "Greetings, favored one! (*Chaire, kecharitomene*)," is very difficult to translate. Spoken in Greek, *Chaire, kecharitomene*, the greeting is very rhythmic and melodious, easy to speak, and pleasing to the ear. At the same time, its wording is very subtle, with a play on words just below the surface. Theologically, the greeting is also extremely meaningful, showing how Mary had been prepared by grace to accept Gabriel's announcement with a whole-hearted *fiat*. All these qualities, including the alliteration, the play on words, and the theology of grace, are lost in most English translations.

Take the rendering, "Greetings, favored one," found in the New Revised Standard Version, or "Hail, favored one," in the Revised

New American Bible. There is very little poetry in "Greetings, favored one," or "Hail, favored one," nothing to suggest a play on words and no hint of the biblical theology of grace. The same can be said of the translation in the Jerusalem Bible, "Rejoice, so highly favored," and in the New Jerusalem Bible, "Rejoice, you who enjoy God's favour."

In English, "Greetings, favored one" or "Hail, favored one" sound archaic, stilted, and somewhat banal, hardly a cause for Mary or anyone to be troubled, let alone greatly troubled. It is also a very poor introduction for the extraordinary announcement that follows. Archaic language is not necessarily elevated.

Admittedly, translating Gabriel's greeting, *Chaire, kecharitomene*, is extremely difficult. The Good News Bible did not even try to translate it. In its place, it substituted another greeting, easier to translate: "Peace be with you."

Not that I have a really good alternative to offer. Much of the loss in rhetorical and literary quality is unavoidable in translation. Alliteration rarely crosses over from one language to another. The same is true for a play on words.

Every translation has its problems, even "Hail, full of grace," from the Latin, *Ave, gratia plena*, which suggests something quantifiable and measurable. But is that a reason to avoid any notion of grace? The Annunciation to Mary is a story of faith. It is also a story of grace.

Later in the story, while responding to Mary's troubled state, Gabriel says: "Do not be afraid, Mary, for you have found favor (*charis*, grace) with God" (1:30). The angel's reference to *charis* (grace) should help us to interpret the second term in the opening greeting, *kecharitomene*, in terms of grace rather than favor. Elsewhere in the New Testament, for example, in the greetings of Paul's letters, "Grace (*charis*) to you and peace," the English translation of *charis* is not "favor" but "grace."[6] It is hard to imagine Paul greeting the early churches with favor and peace: "Favor to you and peace."

A perfect translation may be impossible, but that is no excuse to stop searching. Gabriel's greeting to Mary introduces a mystery, the mystery of the Incarnation. As in all mysteries, mere words are never adequate. That is the way it is with mysteries. Still, it should be possible at least to put the reader in touch with the simplicity, the wonder, and the grace contained in the original.

## "Greetings (*chaire*)"

Gabriel's greeting opens with the word, "greetings" or "hail," in Greek, *chaire*. The word "greetings" is stilted. In English, we no longer use the term, "hail!" as a greeting. By itself, "hail" brings to mind the senior play, *Julius Caesar*, with actors playing at imperial Rome all over school, greeting one another, "Hail, Caesar!" or "Hail, noble Antony!" More than archaic, "hail" sounds artificial.

Still, when the opening word, "hail," is followed by Mary's name, as in "Hail, Mary!" it sounds just fine because we are used to it from the popular prayer of that name, the "Hail Mary." In the New Testament, it was quite normal to greet people by name. We see it, for example, from the third letter of John: "Peace with you. The friends send you their greetings. Greet the friends there, each by name" (3 John 15). Consider also all the people Paul mentions by name when sending greetings at the end of his letters. At the end of the letter to the Romans, Paul greets no less than 26 people by name, beginning with Prisca and Aquila and ending with "Nereus and his sister, and Olympas" (Romans 16:3–16).

Gabriel did not use Mary's name in the greeting. In the context of Luke's story, there was no need, since the name had just been given: "The virgin's name was Mary" (Luke 1:27).[7] That is not the case when the greeting is taken out of Luke's story and made part of a prayer, "Hail Mary." Outside of Luke's narrative context, the name had to be added in order to give personal quality to the prayer.

To prevent Gabriel's word, "greetings" or "hail," from sounding awkward or trivial, all we need do is keep Mary's personal name in mind. In translating and reading the greeting, it is not necessary to speak the name, only to think it.

The Greek imperative, *chaire* ("greetings" or "hail"), was the ordinary greeting used in daily life by Greek-speaking people in New Testament times. When greeting more than one person, people used the plural, *chairete*. Our evidence for this comes from Greek drama and literature, including the New Testament. For example, in Matthew 26:49, Judas approaches Jesus at Gethsemane and greets him: "Greetings, Rabbi!" or "Hail, Rabbi" (*Chaire, hrabbi*). In Matthew 28:9, Jesus greets the women on their way from the tomb: "Greetings" or "Hail" (*Chairete*).[8]

Sometimes, instead of the imperative, the infinitive, *chairein* ("greetings"), was used. The infinitive form, *chairein*, which is more formal, can be found in the opening and closing greetings of countless letters preserved in ancient Egyptian papyri. Literary convention required a more formal greeting. We find *chairein* in the greeting of the letter of James: "To the twelve tribes in the Dispersion: Greetings (*chairein*)" (James 1:1; see Acts 15:23; 23:26).[9]

The early Christians, however, very often did not use the common form, *chaire*. Instead, they greeted one another with a different word, one of great significance theologically, *charis* (grace), which is closely related phonetically to *chaire*. For this we have the evidence of the early Christian letters preserved in the New Testament.

The greeting, *charis*, is found in all the Pauline letters, in the two Petrine letters, as well as in Revelation 1:4, usually combined with *eirene* (peace), as in 1 Thessalonians, "Grace to you and peace" (1 Thessalonians 1:1); sometimes with the further addition of *eleos* (mercy), as in 1 and 2 Timothy, "Grace, mercy and peace" (1 Timothy 1:2; 2 Timothy 1:2).

In most of the letters, the greeting also includes some further theological elaboration, as in 1 Corinthians, "Grace to you and peace from God our Father and the Lord Jesus Christ" (1 Corinthians 1:3). Paul's closing greeting in 2 Corinthians 13:13[10] has become the opening greeting in today's Eucharistic liturgy: "The grace of our Lord Jesus Christ and the love of God and the fellowship of the Holy Spirit be with you all."

The additional reference to "God our Father and the Lord Jesus Christ" reflects the writer's own tendency toward literary and theological elaboration, as well as liturgical influence. Very likely such greetings were used when a church assembled for the Lord's Supper. Knowing that his letters would very likely be read in the assembly, Paul adapted them to the liturgical context.

In the New Testament letters, the simplest form of the grace greeting (*charis*), is found in the closing greetings, as, for example, in Colossians and 1 and 2 Timothy: "Grace be with you" (Colossians 4:18; 1 Timothy 6:21; 2 Timothy 4:22).[11] Presupposing the opening greeting given at the beginning of the letter, the closing greeting shows less tendency toward elaboration. Since literary convention called for greater formality in a letter, very likely the popular greeting used among Greek-speaking Christians was even more simple, namely, "grace" (*charis*).

If the early Christians substituted the greeting *charis* for *chaire*, why would the angel Gabriel in Luke's story have done otherwise? Why did Luke have Gabriel use a common form of greeting instead of a Christian form? An early Christian reader or listener would surely have noted such a departure from tradition. They would also have appreciated the greeting's play on words, using *chaire* for *charis*, reversing the Christian substitution of *charis* for *chaire*.

They would also have recognized the term *charis* included in the participle, *kecharitomene*. If Mary was fully or singularly graced (*kecharitomene*), a greeting wishing her grace (*charis*) would have been redundant. Greeting her with grace, "Grace, fully graced!" would not have made sense.

But what about the meaning of the greeting, *chaire* ("hail" or "greetings")? Some interpreters have stressed the literal meaning of the verb, *chairein* ("rejoice"). As such, the greeting would be a prophetic invitation to messianic joy, as in Zephaniah 3:14, Joel 2:21, and Zechariah 9:9.[12] Zephaniah calls Jerusalem to exult. Its deliverance is at hand:

> *Sing aloud, O daughter Zion!*
> *shout, O Israel!*
> *Rejoice and exult with all your heart,*
> *O daughter Jerusalem!*

Joel calls the very land to rejoice. God's blessing is on her:

> *Do not fear, O soil;*
> *be glad and rejoice,*
> *for the Lord has done great things.*

Zechariah calls Jerusalem to rejoice. Her messianic king is at hand:

> *Rejoice greatly, O daughter Zion!*
> *Shout aloud, O daughter Jerusalem!*
> *Lo, your king comes to you;*
> *triumphant and victorious is he,*
> *humble and riding on a donkey,*
> *on a colt, the foal of a donkey.*

Favoring this interpretation is the fact that the theme of joy (*chara*) is prominent in the annunciation to Zechariah and in the annunciation to the shepherds.[13] Announcing the birth of John, the angel Gabriel says to Zechariah: "You will have joy (*chara*) and gladness, and many will rejoice (*charesontai*) at his birth" (Luke 1:14).

Announcing the birth of Jesus, the angel of the Lord tells the shepherds: "Do not be afraid; for see—I am bringing you good news of great joy (*charan megalen*) for all the people" (2:10). The same prophetic themes are also echoed in Mary's song of praise, the Magnificat (1:46–49):

> My soul magnifies the Lord;
>     and my spirit rejoices (egalliasen) in God my Savior,
> for he has looked with favor on the lowliness of his servant.
>     Surely, from now on all generations will call me blessed;
> For the Mighty One has done great things for me,
>     and holy is his name.

On the other hand, the greeting should not be reduced to the lexical meaning of the verb *chairein*, as we find in the New Jerusalem Bible, "Rejoice, you who enjoy God's favour." In the letter of James, *chairein* (James 1:1) is followed by "Consider it all joy (*pasan charan*), my brothers and sisters, whenever you face trials of any kind, consider it nothing but joy, because you know that the testing of your faith produces endurance" (1:2–3). If *chairein* denoted or even connoted rejoicing, there would have been no need for this exhortation.

More basic is the formal function of the greeting, whose basic purpose is to acknowledge, recognize, and relate to someone personally. Besides, translating *chaire* as "rejoice" distracts from the substitution of *chaire* ("hail") in place of *charis* ("grace") and the transposition of *charis* (grace) into the perfect passive participle *kecharitomene* describing Mary as "fully graced."

Given the solemnity of the greeting, however, we should not reduce it to a common greeting reminiscent of vending stalls and shops in the agora. I suggest that *chaire* includes an intimation of messianic joy, while respecting Gabriel's play on words. In that way, *chaire* opens our minds and hearts to the rest of the greeting and prepares us for the extraordinary announcement that is still coming.

## "Fully Graced (*kecharitomene*)"

Like *chaire* ("greetings"), *kecharitomene* ("favored one") is very difficult to translate. *Kecharitomene* is a perfect passive participle of the
verb *charitoun*, the verbal form of the noun *charis* ("grace" or
"favor"). In the active, *charitoun* means "to grace" or "to favor"
someone; in the passive, "to be graced" or "favored." In the perfect
passive participle, it means "having been graced" or "favored,"[14] with
a nuance of fullness, hence translations like "full of grace," "fully
graced," or "highly favored."

The verb *charitoun* (to confer grace) occurs elsewhere in the
New Testament in Ephesians 1:5–6, "He (God) destined us for
adoption as his children through Jesus Christ, according to the good
pleasure of his will, to the praise of his glorious grace (*eis eplainon
doxes tes charitos autou*) that he freely bestowed (*hes echaritosen,*
favored the grace) on us in the Beloved."

Strictly speaking, the translation "favored one" does render
the meaning of the Greek, *kecharitomene*. Mary surely was greatly
favored by God. But I am not sure that the image of God favoring
someone, presumably not favoring others, or God dispensing favors
is what the greeting should evoke.

The expression "favored one" does not suggest that God's
favor had a transforming effect on Mary, preparing her to accept
the divine commission to conceive in her womb and bring forth
the Son of the Most High. Since the participle is in the passive, it
surely refers to a divine act. Since it is in the perfect, it also refers to
a divine act with enduring effects on Mary, who has been favored
or graced.

In light of the meaning of the perfect tense of the passive participle (*kecharitomene*), I find "full of grace," as we pray in the "Hail
Mary," a better translation than "favored one." It is very hard to
pray: "Hail Mary, favored one, the Lord is with thee."

Surely God's grace had a transforming effect on Mary, making her open to the Holy Spirit and preparing her for a divine commission. The word "grace" does evoke such a transformation. The noun "grace," however, in the expression "full of grace," places all the emphasis on the person of Mary, reinforcing any tendency to leave God out of the picture as well as the purpose for which Mary was graced.

There are two dangers here. One is to stress the effect in Mary at the expense of the divine act, or vice versa. The other is to lose sight of the intention of the divine act and the purpose for which Mary has been graced, namely, to accept to conceive and give birth to the Son of God.

I find the translation "fully graced" more adequate, maintaining a good balance among the various nuances. Better than the noun "grace," the passive of the verb "to grace" (*charitoun*) respects the needed emphasis on God's act in gracing Mary. Like the noun "grace," it also expresses the transformation that has taken place in Mary. It also respects the intention and the purpose of both.[15]

In the greeting, *kecharitomene* replaces Mary's name. Instead of "Hail, Mary," we read "Hail, fully graced." *Kecharitomene* is, therefore, more than a qualitative description of Mary. It is a title, one so close to becoming a name that in Gabriel's greeting it could substitute for a name.[16]

A helpful comparison can be made with Jesus' title *ho Christos* ("the Christ"), which became so identified with Jesus' person that in a relatively short time, *Christos*, without the article, could substitute for Jesus' name. In a further stage, it actually developed into a name. In the New Testament, Jesus, "the Christ," gradually becomes "Jesus Christ," and even more simply, "Christ." Addressing Mary as "fully graced" stands in between, more than a title, but not quite a name.[17]

To appreciate the meaning of "grace" (*charis*) and of being "fully graced" (*kecharitomene*), a comparison with "blessing" (*eulogia*) and being "blessed" (*eulogemene*) can also be very helpful.[18] *Eulogemene* is the greeting Elizabeth used when Mary came to visit her: "Blessed (*eulogemene*) are you among women" (Luke 1:42). Unlike *kecharito-mene*, the participle *eulogemene* is not used as a title.

Ultimately, the blessing comes from God. It is connected with someone's very life, stemming from the person's creation and birth. When God created the human being in the divine image, God created the human being male and female. God then blessed (*eulogesen*) them, saying, "Be fruitful and multiply, and fill the earth and subdue it" (Genesis 1:28). The human being, male and female, was not only a creature. Nor was it the creator. But as male and female, the man and the woman were to be co-creators with God. The purpose of God's blessing was that they might fulfill all the potential that they had as persons from their very creation. For further generations, the potential would stem from their creation and birth.

The normal response to God's blessing is to bless God, asking that God manifest all the potential God has as creator of heaven and earth, as a living God, who is also Lord of history. Blessing God comes very close to the prayer, "Our Father in heaven" or "Father, hallowed be your name, your kingdom come" (Matthew 6:10; Luke 11:2). There is something very daring about blessing God. God just might respond and overwhelm us with the divine potential. While blessing the Lord, we also invite all of creation to join us in the blessing:

> *Sun and moon, bless* (eulogeite) *the Lord* (ton kyrion);
> *praise and exalt him above all forever.*
> *Stars of heaven, bless* (eulogeite) *the Lord* (ton kyrion);
> *praise and exalt him above all forever.*
> (*NAB, Daniel 3:62–63*)

> *Let the earth bless* (eulogeito) *the Lord* (ton kyrion);
> *praise and exalt him above all forever.*
> (*NAB, Daniel 3:74*)

*All you birds of the air, bless* (eulogeite) *the Lord* (ton kyrion);
   *praise and exalt him above all forever.*
*All you beasts, wild and tame, bless* (eulogeite) *the Lord*
      (ton kyrion);
   *praise and exalt him above all forever.*
(*NAB, Daniel 3:80–81*)[19]

Finally, as co-creators, human beings also can bless others, that they might fulfill all the potential that is theirs as human beings from their creation and birth.

Grace is very different. God's gracing of a human being, beginning with Mary, gives new life, together with new potential in view of fulfilling a divine mission. For Mary, being "fully graced" was in view of accepting to conceive and bring forth the Son of the Most High, one who would rule over the house of Jacob forever, transforming the kingdom of David into the kingdom of God (Luke 1:31–33). The story of the Incarnation, including Mary's role in it, is an act of divine grace. From the very beginning, it was all grace.

Similarly, the new life, a "graced" life in Christ, is what makes a Christian the brother or sister to all other Christians, irrespective of ethnic, racial, or national background, and potentially the brother or sister to all human beings. The new potential is to live and act as children of God in the family of God and effectively to announce its gospel.

We can better appreciate the meaning of grace and being graced by considering its normal response, which is very different from the order of blessing. The normal response to God's blessing is to bless God. Not so with grace. There is no gracing God in view of God having new life and new potential. The very thought brings a smile. What then is the normal response to God's grace (*charis*)? It is *eucharistia*, thanksgiving, our word for the Eucharist. When we thank God (*eucharistein*), we mirror back to God the grace (*charis*) of new life and potential.

Reflecting theologically on Mary's *fiat* in this light, we may see it as her response to grace, her incomparable act of thanksgiving. Mary's preparation for conceiving and bringing forth the Son of the Most High is thus both grace (*charis*) and thanksgiving (*eucharistia*). So is the incarnation and its continuation in the sacramental life of the church.

The relationship between *eucharistia* and *charis* can be seen in the thanksgiving passage at the beginning of Paul's letters. We note especially that Paul does not thank those to whom he writes for joining him in the service of the Gospel. Since all grace comes from God, Paul thanks God for those who are partners with him in grace:

> *I thank* (eucharisto) *my God every time I remember you, constantly praying with joy in every one of my prayers for all of you, because of your sharing* (koinonia) *in the gospel from the first day until now . . . you hold me in your heart, for all of you share* (synkoinonous) *in God's grace* (tes charitos) *with me.* (Philippians 1:3–7)

## "The Lord is with You (*ho kyrios meta sou*)"

The angel Gabriel began by greeting Mary, "Hail," addressing her as "fully graced." The angelic greeting concludes with a solemn declaration, "The Lord is with you," a greeting steeped in Old and New Testament theology associated with a long history of divine covenants.

The same greeting, "The Lord is with you," appears only twice in the Old Testament, in Ruth 2:4 and Judges 6:12.[20] In Greek, unlike English, the greeting has no verb. Translated literally, it reads, "The Lord with you." By itself, the greeting is, therefore, quite ambiguous, open to two quite different translations, one as a wish, "The Lord be with you," as in our liturgy, the other as a declaration, "The Lord is with you." The intended meaning must be determined from the context.

In Ruth 2:4, this is how Boaz greeted those harvesting in his field in Bethlehem: "The Lord be with you" (*ho kyrios meta sou*). And the harvesters replied, "The Lord bless you." The parallel response of the harvesters, which is clearly a wish, requires that Boaz' greeting be translated as a wish, "The Lord be with you."

In Judges 6:12, this is how the angel of the Lord greeted Gideon: "The Lord is with you" (*ho kyrios meta sou*). This time, Gideon's response, "If the Lord is with us, why then has all this happened to us?" requires that the greeting be translated as a declaration, "The Lord is with you."

The context of Gabriel's greeting to Mary requires this same translation, "The Lord is with you." Since Mary is "fully graced," the Lord is surely with her. The Lord is with Mary, "fully graced." The declaration states a fact, one which is at the same time a promise. The Lord, who is with Mary, is faithful to his promise. More than a simple declaration, "The Lord is with you" is both a declaration and a proclamation.

"The Lord" (*kyrios*) is more than a title for God (*theos*). In the Septuagint and in the New Testament, it corresponds to the name of God, *Yahweh*, revealed to Moses in Hebrew (Exodus 3:13–15):

> *But Moses said to God, "If I come to the Israelites and say to them, 'The God of your ancestors has sent me to you,' and they ask me, 'What is his name?' what shall I say to them?" God said to Moses, "I AM WHO I AM." He said further, "Thus you shall say to the Israelites: I AM has sent me to you." God also said to Moses, "Thus you shall say to the Israelites, 'The Lord, the God of your ancestors, the God of Abraham, the God of Isaac, the God of Jacob, has sent me to you':*
> > *This is my name forever;*
> > *and this my title for all generations."*

The Greek word for God (*theos*) corresponds to the Hebrew designation, *elohim*. While both of these terms refer to God, they are not interchangeable. "God" is the word for a divine being. "The Lord" is God's name.

"God" (*theos, elohim*) is more generic or abstract. It refers to the God of the universe, to God as the creator, the one who is totally other, but whose existence can be known through philosophical reflection. "The Lord" (*ho kyrios, Yahweh*) refers to God revealing Himself personally, forming a people and being present to them in history, guiding them, nourishing them, whose personal presence can be known only through the experience of faith.

"The Lord," Gabriel said, "is with you,"[21] in solidarity with you, who are fully graced, faithful to the promise contained in that grace. No need to fear.

## But She Was Much Perplexed by His Words

When Mary heard Gabriel's words, "Greetings (hail), favored one (fully graced one)! The Lord is with you" (Luke 1:28), but she was greatly troubled and "much perplexed (*dietarachthe*) and pondered (*dielogizeto*) what sort of greeting this might be" (1:29). When the disciples saw the risen Lord, "they were startled and terrified" (24:37). The Lord Jesus said to them, "Why are you frightened (troubled, *tetaragmenoi*), and why do doubts (*dialogismoi*) arise in your hearts?" (24:38).

There was a reason for Mary to be greatly troubled, as there was other reason for the disciples to be troubled. The disciples "thought that they were seeing (*theorein*) a ghost (*pneuma*, a spirit)" (24:37). There was other reason for Zechariah to be troubled. "When Zechariah saw (*idon*) him (the angel of the Lord), he was terrified (troubled, *etarachthe*);[22] and fear overwhelmed him" (1:12). Mary "was much perplexed (greatly troubled, *dietarachthe*) by his words (*epi to logo*)," the angel Gabriel's greeting (1:29).

The representation of the Annunciation in the twelfth-century window at Chartres depicting the life of Christ catches this precise moment in the story. The angel has just greeted Mary. Mary, standing, her eyes wide open, turned toward the angel, smiling serenely but slightly troubled, holds her right hand raised as in defense but ready to bless.

Zechariah was troubled at the appearance of Gabriel. Mary was greatly troubled, not at Gabriel's appearance, but at the message (*logos*) of Gabriel. In the announcement to Zechariah, Gabriel actually appeared (*ophthe*) to Zechariah. In the announcement to Mary, Gabriel was coming (*eiselthon*) to her, he simply said (*eipen*). Gabriel's appearing to her is never mentioned. All the emphasis is on Gabriel's message.

It is on hearing Gabriel's greeting that Mary was deeply troubled. The greeting, "Hail, fully graced, the Lord is with you," was but an introduction for Gabriel's announcement. So extraordinary a greeting implied something absolutely awesome was about to be announced. Mary would have a part in it, so far undisclosed. The greeting also said a lot about Mary. What would be asked of her? What would be asked of a lowly virgin? Identifying with Mary, we too feel deeply troubled.

## And Pondered What Sort of Greeting This Might Be

Deeply troubled at Gabriel's greeting, Mary pondered (*dielogizeto*) what the greeting (*aspasmos*) might be. Not that she had difficulty understanding the words, but what did the words really say? What did they imply? Such pondering takes time, the kind of time needed for reflection, meditation and contemplation.[23]

While Mary was pondering the angel's greeting, she was pondering the shepherds' visit: "But Mary treasured all these words and pondered them in her heart" (2:19).[24]

Mary saw the shepherds at the manger in Bethlehem:

*So they (the shepherds) went in haste and found Mary and Joseph, and the infant lying in the manger. When they saw this,*

*they made known what had been told them about this child; and*
*who all heard it were amazed at what the shepherds told them.*
*(2:16–18)*

Mary listened to the shepherds' message that the angel had
proclaimed to them:

*Do not be afraid; for see (behold, idou), I am bringing you good*
*news (euaggelizomai) of great joy for all the people: to you is*
*born this day in the city of David a Savior, who is the Messiah,*
*the Lord. This will be a sign for you: you will find a child wrapped*
*in bands of cloth and lying in a manger. (2:10–12)*

Identifying with Mary, we ponder the greeting with her, over
two thousand years after the event, over nineteen hundred years
after its story was told. "Hail, fully graced. The Lord is with you"
(1:28). Who would not be troubled at such a greeting? Who could
dismiss such an extraordinary greeting without wondering and
pondering what it implied?

Why did the angel Gabriel come to Mary? Why was Mary
fully graced? Why was God with her? To answer those questions, we
also must ponder Mary's role in the history of salvation. We must
also read on and hear Gabriel's announcement.

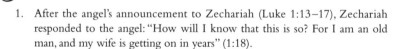

1.   After the angel's announcement to Zechariah (Luke 1:13–17), Zechariah
     responded to the angel: "How will I know that this is so? For I am an old
     man, and my wife is getting on in years" (1:18).

2.   In Matthew, the angel of the Lord appeared in a dream to Joseph, but not to
     announce that Mary would conceive and bear him a son. Mary had already
     conceived. After her conception, the angel appeared to Joseph to announce
     that Mary had conceived through the Holy Spirit (Matthew 1:18–25).

3.   "Jesus said to her, 'Mary !' She turned and said to him in Hebrew (*Hebraisti*)
     '*Rabbouni!*' (which means Teacher [*Didaskale*])" (John 20:16). The term

*Rabbouni*, a Greek transliteration of Aramaic, means "my master" or "my teacher."

4. See also John 20:19, 21. A similar greeting is found in the Lord's instructions to the seventy: "Whatever house you enter, first say, 'Peace to this house'" (Luke 10:5).

5. Both Luke and Acts include great journey narratives, contributing significantly to their structure. In Luke, the journey is geographically to Jerusalem, thematically to the Ascension, when Jesus fulfills the promise made to Abraham that in his progeny all the families of the earth would be blessed (Luke 9:51–24:53). In Acts, the journey is to Rome, symbolic of "the ends of the earth" (Acts 1:8) giving gospel access to all peoples (19:21—28:31).

6. The greetings of the Pauline letters translate in the New Revised Standard Version, New American Bible, and the New Jerusalem Bible from the Greek *charis* to the English "grace."

7. The difference between the greeting in the annunciation to Zechariah and the Annunciation to Mary is considerable. When the angel of the Lord appeared to him, "he (Zechariah) was terrified; and fear overwhelmed him" (Luke 1:12). It was only then that Gabriel greeted him, using his name: "Do not be afraid, Zechariah" (1:13). When the angel Gabriel comes to Mary, no initial reaction on her part is given. Instead, Gabriel greets her from the start. Mary then reacts to the greeting itself, not, unlike Zechariah, to the vision.

8. The greeting is only referred to, not translated, in the Revised New American Bible: "And behold, Jesus met them on their way and greeted them" (Matthew 28:9); in the New Revised Standard Version: "Suddenly Jesus met them and said, 'Greetings! (*Xairete*)'" (Matthew 28:9).

9. For the simple greeting, *chairein*, also the letters of Ignatius of Antioch, where we find *pleista chairein*, "abundant greetings."

10. The translation of the New Revised Standard Version is "The grace of the Lord Jesus Christ, the love of God, and the communion of the Holy Spirit be with all of you" (2 Corinthians 13:13).

11. In the closing greeting, Paul refers to grace (*charis*) except in Romans 15:3, where the greeting is *eirene* (peace).

12. S. Lyonnet, SJ, "*Chaire kecharitomene*," *Biblica* 20 (1939) 131–141; Jean-Paul Audet, OP, "*L'annonce a Marie*," *Revue Biblique* 63 (1956) 346–374, esp. 357–358.

13. For a critique of this position, see Raymond E. Brown, SS, *The Birth of the Messiah*, (New York: Doubleday, 1993), 321–324, 631.

14. For the perfect participle passive verb, see Maximilian Zerwick, SJ, *Biblical Greek* (Rome: Scripta Pontificii Instituti Biblici, 1963) 96, no. 285, "In essence, though not exactly in use, the Greek perfect tense corresponds to the English

one, in that it is not a past tense but a present one, indicating not the past action as such but the present 'state of affairs' resulting from the past action."

15. For a discussion of these issues, together with the expression's background, see Ignace de la Potterie, SJ, "*Kecharitomene en Lc 1,28; Etude philologique*," *Biblica* 68 (1987) 357–382, and its continuation in "Etude exegetique et theologique," *Biblica* 68 (1987) 480–508. On Luke 1:28, with others, I agree that de la Potterie emphasizes the Mariological aspect, the effect in Mary, at the expense of the theological and Christological aspect. For a response, see Brown, *The Birth of the Messiah*, 325–327, 631–635.

16. See Joseph A. Fitzmyer, SJ, *The Gospel According to Luke I–IX*, Anchor Bible 28 (New York: Doubleday, 1981): "This phrase functions here almost as a proper name; cf. Judg 6:12 for a similar use of an epithet," 345.

17. See the encyclical letter of John Paul II on the Annunciation of Our Lord (March 25, 1987), *Mother of the Redeemer* (*Redemptoris Mater*), trans. Vatican: "For the messenger greets Mary as "full of grace"; he calls her thus as if it were her real name. He does not call her by her proper earthly name Miryam (= Mary), but *by this new name: "full of grace.*" Part I, "Mary in the Mystery of Christ," 1, "Full of Grace," 8 (Boston: Daughters of St. Paul, 1987) 13.

18. In the first story of the breaking of the bread (Mark 6:34–44), Mark "used the Greek verb *eulogein* (to bless, 6:41) and not *eucharistein* (to give thanks) that is used in his second story of the breaking of the bread (8:6). Beneath these two Greeks verbs lies the single Hebrew verb *barak*, which includes both notions and shows how closely they were related. Even today, we may thank someone by responding, "Bless you." See E. LaVerdiere, *The Beginning of the Gospel, Introducing the Gospel According to Mark* (Collegeville: The Liturgical Press, 1999) 1:175–176, 210; 2:236–238.

19. See Daniel 3:52–90. Shadrach, Meshach, and Abednego in the fiery furnace "with one voice sing, glorifying and blessing God" (Daniel 3:51). They sing the canticle of praise. These verses in Daniel 3:24–90 are inspired additions to the Aramaic text of Daniel, including the prayer of Azariah (3:24–45) and the hymn of Shadrach, Meshach, and Abednego (3:46–90). The verses are in the Septuagint (Greek) and the Vulgate (Latin). The verses are not in the Masoretic Text (Hebrew) and New Revised Standard Version. The Roman Catholic Church has always regarded them as part of the canonical scriptures.

20. The same or a similar expression is used outside a greeting formula, for example, in 1 Chronicles 22:11, 16.

21. As revealed to Moses, the name of God, I AM, does not simply refer to God's existence. It says "I AM with you." The closing element in Gabriel's greeting, "The Lord is with you," simply spells out the implied of the divine name.

22. Elsewhere in Luke, Luke uses the passive voice of the verb *tarrasso* (be troubled) in 24:38. In Acts, he uses the active voice (to trouble) in 15:24; 17:8, 13.

23. Besides here in 1:29, Luke uses the term *dialogizomai* (to ponder) in 3:15; 5:21, 22; 12:17; 20:14. He uses the noun *dialogismos* (thought, thinking, pondering) in 2:35; 5:22; 6:8; 9:46, 47; 24:38.

24. After Mary and Joseph found Jesus in the temple of Jerusalem (2:41–50), "Then he (Jesus) went down with them and came to Nazareth, and was obedient to them. His mother treasured all these things in her heart" (2:51).

# The Angel's Announcement to Mary

*The angel said to her,*
*"Do not be afraid, Mary,*
*for you have found favor with God.*
*And now,*
*you will conceive in your womb and bear a son,*
*and you will name him Jesus.*
*He will be great and will be called*
*the Son of the Most High,*
*and the Lord God will give to him*
*the throne of his ancestor David.*
*He will reign over the house of Jacob forever,*
*and of his kingdom there will be no end."*
*(Luke 1:30–33)*

We have now come to the very heart of the story, to the Annunciation itself. With the announcement, we also enter the second phase in the dialogue between the angel Gabriel and the virgin Mary (1:30–34).

After quieting Mary's fear, Gabriel announces that Mary would conceive and bear a son who will be called the Son of the Most High (Luke 1:30–33). In response, Mary asks how this would be since she had no relations with a man (1:34).

We saw how in the sixth month of Elizabeth's pregnancy of John, the angel Gabriel was sent from (*apo*) God to a city (*eis polin*) of Galilee named Nazareth, to a humble virgin engaged to a man named Joseph, who was of the house of David. The virgin's name was Mary (1:26–27).

Earlier, Gabriel appeared to a priest named Zechariah while he was offering incense in the sanctuary of the Lord. Zechariah was troubled (*etarachthe*) by what he saw (*idon*) and was struck with fear (*phobos*). Greeting him, Gabriel responded to Zechariah's fear: "Do not be afraid (*me phobou*), Zechariah, because your prayer has been heard" (1:13).

Zechariah had nothing to fear. Gabriel came with good news (1:19). His wife, Elizabeth, would bear him a son, whose name would be John (1:13).

Now, six months later, Gabriel was sent to a virgin named Mary. Unlike the annunciation to Zechariah, the Annunciation to Mary does not indicate where Mary was or what she was doing when the angel Gabriel came to her. Perhaps Mary was at prayer (see Acts 1:14). Probably, she was attentive to the word of God (see 8:21). In their interpretation, many artists show Mary in a room at home at a prie-dieu with the book of the scriptures in her hand or the scriptures open before her.

Since Mary had found grace before God (Luke 1:28, 30), she was surely in the presence of God, wherever she was and whatever she was doing.

We saw later that Mary had not reacted when she saw the angel Gabriel coming to her (1:28a), unlike Zechariah who reacted when he saw Gabriel appearing to him: "Then there appeared to him an angel of the Lord. . . . When Zechariah saw him, he was terrified; and fear overwhelmed him" (1:11–12).

When Gabriel was sent to Zechariah, the story immediately focused on Zechariah, describing him as troubled and fearful.

Zechariah's reaction set the tone for Gabriel's response: "Do not be afraid, Zechariah, for your prayer has been heard" (1:13).

When Gabriel is sent to Mary, the story focuses on Gabriel's greeting: "Greetings (hail, *chaire*), favored one (fully graced, *kecharitomene*)! The Lord is with you (*ho kyrios meta sou*)" (1:28). Gabriel's greeting sets the tone for Mary's response, which is then described as greatly troubled (1:29).

Unlike Zechariah, Mary was not troubled at the presence of Gabriel. Nor was she fearful at the angel's appearance. What troubled her was Gabriel's greeting. It is only after hearing the angel's word (*epi to logo*) that Mary was greatly troubled (*dietarachthe*) and pondered (*dielogizeto*) what kind of greeting (*aspasmos*) this might be (1:29).

In the whole course of biblical history, no one had ever been greeted in this way: "Greetings, favored one (fully graced)."

People had been blessed. Abraham had been singularly blessed (Genesis 12:2–3). Isaac had also been blessed (26:24). And Jacob had been blessed (35:10–12). Indeed, the whole human race had been blessed in the primeval couple (1:28). No one, however, had ever been graced, fully graced (*kecharitomene*), as Mary was called.

If Mary was fully graced, it was for a purpose. Gabriel's greeting spoke of Mary's privileged position in relation to God, a graced relationship in view of her special role in the history of salvation. For a mere virgin from a city in Galilee, it was all very troubling. What would Mary's role be? What would she be expected to do? So far, it had not been revealed.

More important, Gabriel's greeting to Mary implied that something extraordinary was about to happen, an event in which Mary would play an essential role but whose significance would far transcend her role. It was not for her own sake that Mary was fully graced, not for her sake that the Lord was with her. It was in view of an event greater than all of God's previous wonders and signs, surpassing every previous expectation.

Mary was fully graced. The Lord was with her. That was something to ponder. What might God have in store for her? What might God have in store for the human race? So far, it had not been announced.

The participants, the angel Gabriel and the virgin Mary, have been introduced (1:26–27). The angel Gabriel has greeted Mary, and Mary's troubled reaction has been noted (1:28–29). It is time for Gabriel's announcement to Mary (1:30–33).

Gabriel's announcement comes in three parts. In the first part (1:30), Gabriel responded to Mary's reaction to Gabriel's greeting (*epi to logo*):

> *Do not be afraid, Mary,*
> *for you have found favor (grace, charin) with God.*

This first part concerns Mary herself. As such, it is relating to the traditional form of a commissioning story.

Quieting Mary's fear, Gabriel referred to the opening greeting: "Greetings, favored (fully graced) one! The Lord is with you" (1:28). As singularly graced (*ke**chari**tomene*), Mary has found grace (*charin*) before God (*para¹ to theo*). She has no reason to fear.

In this first part of the announcement (1:30), Gabriel is preparing Mary to receive the rest of the announcement, that she will conceive and bear a son, the Son of the Most High (1:31–33). The second part and third part relate to the traditional form of an announcement story.

The second part of the announcement (1:31) concerns Mary and her son, named Jesus:

> *And now (idou),*
> *you will conceive in your womb and bear a son,*
> *and you will name him Jesus.*

As such, the second part serves as an introduction (1:31) for the third part of the announcement (1:32–33). The third part (1:32–33) concerns Jesus, the Son of the Most High and the Davidic Messiah:

> He will be great and will be called the Son of the Most High, and the Lord God will give to him the throne of his ancestor David. He will reign over the house of Jacob forever, and of his kingdom there will be no end.

After a brief introduction (first part) giving Gabriel's response to Mary (1:30), the announcement comes in two parts (second and third parts). The second announces that Mary would conceive in her womb and bear a son, whom she would name Jesus. This second part is related to Mary's role as the mother of Jesus (1:31).

The third part announces the greatness of Jesus, how he would be called the Son of the Most High, how the Lord God would give to him the throne of his ancestor David, how he would rule over the house of Jacob forever, and how his kingdom would be without end. Jesus would fulfill the history of salvation. This third part is related to the identity and mission of Jesus (1:32–33).

## "Do Not Be Afraid, Mary, for You Have Found Favor with God" (1:30)

Then the angel said to her, "Do not be afraid (*me phobou*), Mary, for (*gar*) you have found favor (grace, *charin*) with God" (1:30). Gabriel began by reassuring Mary. Like Zechariah, Mary had no grounds for fearing. In Zechariah's case, that was because (*dioti*) Zechariah's prayer had been heard (1:13). In Mary's case, for (*gar*) Mary had found grace before God.

Telling Mary, "Do not be afraid," Gabriel recalls how he greeted Mary on coming to her: "Greetings (hail, *chaire*)." Sometimes, the angel of the Lord came in judgment. Not in Mary's case, as the greeting made clear. Continuing, Gabriel then explained how

Mary came to be *kecharitomene* (fully graced): "for you have found favor (*charin*, grace) with God." But to know what the word (*logos*) of Gabriel was about, Mary had to wait for the actual announcement. Only then would she know why she was singularly graced and why the Lord was with her.

It was quite normal for Mary to be troubled, indeed deeply troubled, by Gabriel's greeting. It was also quite normal for Gabriel to reassure Mary and dispel what was troubling her. That is the way it is when the Lord God or the angel of the Lord calls someone for a special role in history.

The expression, "Do not be afraid," is not part of the Old Testament literary pattern for stories announcing a significant birth.[2] However, we do find the expression, "Do not be afraid," in four stories of the New Testament, announcing either the birth of Jesus (Luke 1:26–38; 2:8–14; Matthew 1:18–25) or that of John the Baptist (1:5–25). In each case, the expression does not have to do with the announcement itself, that is, with the birth of Jesus or John the Baptist, but with the person who receives the announcement and is given a special role regarding it.

The reason Mary had no need to fear is that she had found grace (*charin*) before God (1:30b). The reason Zechariah had no need to fear is that the angel of the Lord had come to announce good news (*euaggelisasthai*, 1:19). His prayer had been heard (1:13). The reason the shepherds had no need to fear is that the angel appeared (*epeste*) to them to proclaim good news (*euaggelizomai*) of great joy that would be for all the people (2:10).

In Luke, the fear of Zechariah, Mary, and the shepherds is related either to the angel's appearance and presence or the angel's greeting. In Matthew's Gospel, however, it has nothing to do with the angel of the Lord, who appeared to Joseph in a dream. It has to do with the situation confronting Joseph. Before he lived with her, Mary, his wife, was found with child. The angel of the Lord tells

Joseph not to be afraid to take Mary his wife into his home, "for the child conceived in her is from the Holy Spirit" (Matthew 1:20).

The Old Testament background for the expression, "Do not be afraid," comes from stories of Abraham and Isaac in Genesis and God's promise of posterity to them. First, "the word of the Lord came to Abram in a vision: 'Do not be afraid, Abram, I am your shield; your reward shall be very great'" (Genesis 15:1). Abram had no need to fear. His future was assured. God promised him a great posterity, descendants as numerous as the stars (15:2–6). God also promised him a land as his own possession (15:7–8), and God and Abram sealed the promise in a covenant (15:9–21).

A story about Isaac may be even more significant: "And that very night the Lord (*kyrios*) appeared (*ophthe*) to him and said, 'I am (*ego eimi*) the God of your father Abraham: do not be afraid (*me phobou*), for I am with you (*meta sou gar eimi*) and will bless you and make your offspring numerous for my servant Abraham's sake'" (26:24).

Isaac had no need to fear because God was with him. Like Isaac, Mary had no need to fear. The Lord was with her (*ho kyrios meta sou*).

The Book of Jeremiah says much the same about Jacob in two closely related texts. Jacob has no need to fear (30:10–11):

> But as for you, have no fear, my servant Jacob, says the Lord,
>     and do not be dismayed, O Israel;
> for I am going to save you from far away,
>     and your offsprings from the land of their captivity.
> Jacob shall return and have quiet and ease,
>     And no one shall make him afraid.
> For I am with you, says the Lord, to save you.

Later, Jacob is again told (46:28):

*As for you, have no fear, my servant Jacob, says the Lord,*
*for I am with you.*

Like Jacob, Mary must not fear. She has found favor (*charin*, grace) with God (*para to theo*). The Lord will be with her as she fulfills the role that Gabriel is about to announce.

## "And Now (behold, *kai idou*)" (1:31a)

At the beginning of the story, the focus was on Gabriel, until Mary was introduced (Luke 1:26–27). From that point on, the focus was on the virgin, Mary, greeted as "favored one (fully graced, *kecharitomene*)," on her troubled state and how Gabriel reassured her (1:28–30).

With the expression, "And now (behold,[3] *kai idou*)" (1:31a), the focus shifts for a second time. In a biblical narrative, "And now (behold, *kai idou*)" has several functions. Rhetorically, it calls attention to what immediately follows. As a narrative device, it also indicates a shift in perspective.[4] As a traditional biblical expression, it invests a story with biblical resonance.

The expression, "behold," has a long history in the Old Testament, both in Hebrew (*hinneh*) and in Greek (*idou*). From the Old Testament, it entered the New, evoking an ancient, biblical atmosphere. Even in English, "behold" sounds biblical. It also sounds archaic and stilted, as does the greeting, "hail."

That must not distract us from the expression's principal function, which is to signal a new point of view. To help in that, we might translate *idou*, or at least think of *idou*, as "Look!"[5] or "Listen!" After Gabriel quieted Mary's fear, he said to her: "Look, you will conceive in your womb and bear a son, and you will name him Jesus" (1:31); "Listen, you will conceive in your womb and bear a son. . . . He (Jesus) will be great and will be called the Son of the

Most High" (1:32a). "Listen!" Listening intently, Mary heard Gabriel's message!

When Gabriel greeted Mary, the point of view was that of Gabriel coming and speaking to Mary. Within the story, the word "behold" draws Mary's attention away from Gabriel's greeting and focuses it on the substance of Gabriel's message as the words begin to take shape before her eyes. Gabriel's "behold" does the same thing for the readers, who are made to redirect their eyes toward what Mary sees.

Until now, we saw Mary through the eyes of Gabriel. Joining Mary, we then heard Gabriel's greeting. Troubled, we joined Mary as she pondered. With "behold," the perspective shifts, and we begin seeing through Mary's eyes. With her we focus on her commission to conceive and bring forth a son (1:31). With her we see Gabriel's message concerning her son, Jesus, who would be great and called Son of the Most High. We also see Jesus' role in the history of salvation (1:32–33).

## "You Will Conceive in Your Womb and Bear a Son" (1:31b)

From the start, there is a certain awkwardness and redundance about the announcement. Would it not have been sufficient to say, "You will conceive (*syllempse*),"[6] without specifying "in your womb (*en gastri*)"? Besides, was it really necessary to distinguish between conceiving and bearing a son (*texe huion*)?

The announcement of the birth of John the Baptist to Zechariah was much simpler: "Your wife Elizabeth will bear you a son (*gennesei huion soi*), and you will name him John" (1:13). The announcement to Zechariah was patterned on the announcement to Abraham regarding the birth of Isaac: "No, but your wife Sarah shall bear you a son (*texetai soi huion*), and you shall name him Isaac" (Genesis 17:19a).

The awkwardness disappears when we recognize that these expressions in Gabriel's announcement come from the Old Testament. From its opening words, the announcement of Jesus' conception and birth is clothed in traditional, biblical language, associating Jesus' conception and birth with Old Testament stories announcing the conception and birth of a son.

We recall especially the words of the angel of the Lord to Hagar announcing the birth of Ishmael (Genesis 16:11):

> *Now (behold, idou)*
> *you have conceived (LXX, in your womb, en gastri),*
> *and shall bear a son (kai texe huion);*
> *you shall call his name Ishmael*
> (kai kaleseis to onoma autou Ismael).

We also recall the words of the angel of the Lord to the mother of Samson (*Judges 13:3, see 5 and 7*):

> *Although you are barren,*
> *   have borne no children,*
> *you shall conceive (LXX, in your womb, en gastri)*
> *and bear a son (kai texe huion).*

Later, we are told, "and named him Samson (*kai ekalesen to onoma autou Sampson*" (Judges 13:24).

And of course there are the oracular words of Isaiah, announcing the birth of the future king Hezekiah (Isaiah 7:14):

> *Hear then, O house of David!* . . .
> *Therefore the Lord himself will give you a sign.*
> *Look, the young woman (LXX, behold the virgin, idou*
> he parthenos)
> *is with child (LXX, shall conceive in her womb, en gastri hexei)*
> *and shall bear a son (kai texetai huion),*

*and (you) shall name him Immanuel*
*(LXX, and you [Ahaz, king of Judah] shall call*
*his name Emmanuel,*
kai kaleseis to onoma autou Emmanouel).

In light of these Old Testament passages and the Septuagintal background that at first seem awkward, the announcement to Mary is given a rich biblical tone, inviting readers to situate the announcement in the biblical context. With that, what also seemed redundant brings a poetic quality to the announcement. It also associates Jesus' conception and birth with biblical hope, which would now be fulfilled in Jesus' life and mission.

## "And You Will Name Him Jesus" (1:31c)

After conceiving in her womb and bearing a son, Mary, not Joseph, would call her son Jesus (*kaleseis onoma autou Iesoun*).[7] In the same way, as we have just seen, it was Hagar, not Abraham, who would call her son's name Ishmael (Genesis 16:11). It was also the mother of Samson who would name him (Judges 13:24), and in the Hebrew text of Isaiah, it is the virgin who would name him Immanuel (Isaiah 7:14). In the Septuagint, however, it is not the virgin but Ahaz, king of Judah, who is to call the virgin's son Emmanuel (7:14).

Normally, it was the father's role to designate the name of the child. Recall how in the case of John the Baptist, it was Zechariah who was expected to name him John: "And you (Zechariah) will name him John" (Luke 1:13). In this respect, the announcement to Zechariah was patterned on the announcement to Abraham regarding the birth of Isaac: "and you shall call his name Isaac" (Genesis 17:19).

At this point, Gabriel's message to Mary is more than an announcement of what is about to unfold. Telling Mary that she will name her son Jesus is also a part of her commission. But what precisely is the nature of the request? Mary's role is only to confer the name. She is not the one who chooses the name. Jesus' name was given to her by the angel Gabriel, who brought it with him when he came from God.

In the biblical world, a person's name speaks the person's identity. To give someone a name is to determine someone's identity. To change someone's name is to change the person's identity and role in life.[8] Jesus' identity came from God. So did the good news of his birth to the shepherds (Luke 2:9–11). And so did Jesus' name come from the angel Gabriel, ultimately from God.

It is the Father, the Most High, who determined and gave Jesus his name. In conferring the name, Mary, virgin and mother, was the Father's instrument. That is why, after Jesus was born, when the time came to give Jesus his name, the event is told in the passive. Instead of saying, "She (Mary) named him Jesus," Luke relates:

> *After eight days had passed, it was time to circumcise the child;*
> *and he was called* (eklethe) *Jesus, the name given him by the*
> *angel before he was conceived in the womb.* (2:21)

When John the Baptist was born, Zechariah had a much greater role in determining the name of John. When people were going to call his son Zechariah, he wrote what he wished him to be called: "His name is John" (1:59–63).

At first, Zechariah had doubted the message of the angel of the Lord (Gabriel): "How will I know that this is so? For I am an old man, and my wife is getting on in years" (1:18). Gabriel replied: "But now, because you did not believe my words, which will be fulfilled in their time, you will become mute, unable to speak, until the day these things occur" (1:20). After the birth of John, now he obeyed: "He asked for a tablet and wrote, 'His name is John'" (1:63).

## "He Will Be Great and Will Be Called
## the Son of the Most High" (1:32a)

In the second part of the announcement (1:31), the angel focused on Mary, the virgin of Nazareth, saying that she would conceive and bear a son, whom she would name Jesus. In this second part, Gabriel's announcement included the elements of commission. As an announcement, Gabriel's message was a revelation from God, communicated to Mary. As a commission, Gabriel's message was an invitation from God, directed to Mary. It is for this that Mary was fully graced. The Lord was with her (1:28–29). She had no reason to fear. She had found grace before God (1:30).

In the third part of the announcement (1:32–33), the angel focuses entirely on Jesus, saying that Jesus will be great and on the role he will play in the history of salvation. The biblical atmosphere set in the second part continues throughout this third part, where each expression is richly evocative of biblical expectation.

After Gabriel's greeting, and Mary's reaction, and Gabriel's reassuring words, "Do not be afraid, Mary, for you have found favor (grace, *charin*) with God," we expect something extraordinary. For a virgin to conceive, however, and bear a son, and give him the name Jesus does not seem so extraordinary. Something similar happens every time a young woman, or a virgin, conceives for the first time after having relations with a man. For the young woman herself, the announcement may be quite extraordinary, but not for others, let alone for the whole human race. Even in Nazareth, it would not have been extraordinary.

For such an announcement, it would not have been necessary for Gabriel to be sent from God. Gabriel, we recall, is the one who would come to announce the imminent fulfillment of the people's eschatological hopes and dreams.

Even from the first part of the announcement (1:31) we also expect more, something at least in the order of a Judge like Samson

(Judges 13:3, 5, 7, 24), someone who would stand in the ancestral line of Abraham, Isaac and Jacob (Genesis 16:11), or a king like Hezekiah (Isaiah 7:14), perhaps even a royal messiah from the house of David.

But Mary conceiving in her womb, bearing a son, and giving him the name Jesus is only the second part of the announcement. The high point comes in the third part. As in the case of Samson, Ishmael, and Hezekiah, the announcement now presents the identity and describes the mission of Jesus. Who would this child be? Everything in the story has been pointing to this moment.

Mary was singularly graced and the Lord was with her (Luke 1:28). Mary had found grace with God (1:30) so that she would be able to accept Gabriel's announcement to conceive and bear not just any son, but this particular son.

To appreciate Gabriel's announcement concerning Jesus, Mary's son, we should compare it to Gabriel's announcement concerning John, the son of Zechariah and Elizabeth.

John would "be great (*megas*) in the sight of the Lord" (1:15a). Set aside for the Lord's service, "He must never drink wine or strong drink" (1:15b), like Samson (Judges 13:4–5) and Samuel (1 Samuel 1:11, LXX). John's greatness would be shown in his mission as "the prophet of the Most High," going "before the Lord to prepare his ways" (Luke 1:76).

Jesus too would "be great (*megas*)." He would "be called the Son of the Most High" (1:32a). John would be great as the prophet of the Most High. Jesus would be great as the Son of the Most High.[9]

In today's context, the passive, "be called the Son of the Most High," is open to misunderstanding, as though Jesus was not actually the Son of the Most High but merely called such. In the biblical context, however, including the New Testament, such a passive is often theological. Jesus would "be called the Son of the Most High" by the Lord God.

God called Jesus "my Son, the Beloved" (3:22), and "my Son, my Chosen" (9:35). We see this later on in Luke's Gospel in the story of Jesus' Baptism: "And a voice came from heaven, 'You are my Son, the Beloved; with you I am well pleased'" (3:22), and again at Jesus' Transfiguration, "Then from the cloud came a voice that said, 'This is my Son, my Chosen; listen to him'" (9:35).

## "And the Lord God Will Give to Him the Throne of His Ancestor David" (1:32b)

The Lord God would also give Jesus, the Son of the Most High, the throne of David his father (1:32b). Like the title, "the Son of the Most High," the "Son of David" (18:38–39; 20:41; Matthew 21:9; Mark 11:9–10) is a messianic title.[10]

Gabriel's announcement concerning Jesus (1:32b) refers to the prophet Nathan's announcement concerning David's son: "I (the Lord) will raise up your offspring after you" (2 Samuel 7:12b). The Lord gave the message to Nathan for King David (7:12–16):

> *When your days are fulfilled and you lie down with your ancestors, I (the Lord) will raise up your offspring after you (David), who shall come forth from your body, and I will establish his kingdom. He shall build a house for my name,[11] and I will establish the throne of his kingdom forever. I will be a father to him, and he shall be a son to me. . . . Your house and your kingdom shall be made sure forever before me; your throne shall be established forever.*

Later, after the deportation to Babylon, when Israel was without a king, that message would acquire royal messianic implication.[12]

Nathan's oracle provided the theological basis of Israelite and Jewish royal messianism. Here in the story of the Annunciation to Mary, it underlies Gabriel's announcement concerning Jesus.

Like Jesus, who was called the Son of the Most High, David too had been designated a son of God: "I (the Lord) will be a father to him, and he (David) shall be a son to me" (2 Samuel 7:14; 1 Chronicles 17:13; 22:10; 28:6). The Lord would be an adoptive father, and David would be an adopted son. As such, the Lord would show a Father's care toward him, and he would respond with filial obedience. Should he do evil and disobey, the Lord would punish his adopted son but would not abandon him.

As Gabriel said, Jesus would be David's son and be given the throne of David his father. Like David, Jesus would also be the Son of God, but unlike David, Jesus would be more than God's adopted son. As "the Son of the Most High," he would enjoy divine life in an absolutely unique way, fulfilling Nathan's oracle, as others had done, but beyond every expectation.

More than God's adoptive son, Jesus would be God's only Son by nature. There is a difference in the capital of "Son" and the minuscule "a son." Jesus is the Son of the Most High. David is a son of God.

In the Sermon on the Plain (Luke 6:35; see Matthew 5:44–45), Jesus said to the disciples:

> But love your enemies, do good, and lend, expecting nothing
> in return. Your reward will be great, and you will be children
> (huioi, *sons and daughters*) *of the Most High* (hypsistou);
> *for he is kind to the ungrateful and the wicked.*

Now, we are the disciples of Jesus. Now, if we love our enemies, we are the sons and daughters of the Most High!

Jesus spells it out while teaching in the temple. Jesus had just responded (20:34–38) to the Sadducees' question about the resurrection (20:27–33). Since "they (the Sadducees) no longer dared to ask him (Jesus) another question" (20:40), Jesus had a question for the Sadducees (20:41–44):

*"How do they say that the Messiah is David's son?*
*For David himself says in the book of Psalms,*[13]
*'The Lord said to my Lord,*
*"Sit at my right hand* (ek dexion mou)
*until I make your enemies your footstool."'*
*David thus calls him Lord; so how can he be his son?"*

As the Son of the Most High, Jesus, the Son of David, would transcend the Davidic line while fulfilling it.[14]

In Jesus' Passion, the elders of the people, chief priests, and
scribes brought Jesus before their Sanhedrin. They said: "If you are
the Messiah, tell us" (22:66–67a). Jesus replied, "If I tell you, you
will not believe; and if I question you, you will not answer. But from
now on the Son of Man will be seated at the right hand (*ek dexion*)
of the power of God" (22:67b–69; see Mark 14:62; Matthew 26:64).

Jesus will be raised from the tomb. As Lord Jesus, he will sit at
the Lord God's right hand. At Pentecost, Peter preached to the
Israelites that Jesus is exalted at the right hand of God (Acts 2:32–35):

*"This Jesus God raised up, and of that all of us are witnesses.*
*Being therefore exalted at the right hand of God* (te dexia ouv
tou theou hypsotheis). . . . *For David did not ascend into*
*the heavens, but he himself says,*
*'The Lord said to my Lord,*
*"Sit at my right hand* (ek dexion mou)
*until I make your enemies*
*your footstool."'"*

God's "right hand" is the image of power, life and salvation.
According to Exodus, Moses and the Israelites sang the canticle to
the Lord, singing that the right hand of the Lord God is a symbol
of power (15:3–6):

*The Lord is a warrior,*
　　*the Lord is his name.*
*Pharoah's chariots and his army he cast into the sea;*
　　*his picked officers were sunk in the Red Sea.*
*The floods covered them;*
　　*they went down into the depths like a stone.*
*Your right hand* (he dexia sou), *O Lord, glorious in power—*
　　*your right hand* (he dexia sou cheir),
*O Lord, shattered the enemy.*

According to Psalm 138, we sing that the right hand of the Lord God is a symbol of life and salvation (138:7; LXX, Psalm 137:7):

*Though I walk in the midst of trouble,*
*you preserve me against the wrath of my enemies;*
*you stretch out your hand* (cheiras sou),
*and your right hand* (he dexia sou)
*delivers* (esose, *saves*) *me.*

## "He Will Reign over the House of Jacob Forever, and of His Kingdom There Will Be No End" (1:33)

The Lord God will give Jesus the throne of David his father. From the throne of David, Jesus will rule over the house of Jacob forever.

In the Old Testament, the name of Jacob is a common designation for Israel. The house of Jacob is the house of Israel. In Deuteronomy, Moses said the words of this song (32:8–9):

*When the Most High apportioned the nations,*
　　*when he divided humankind,*
*he fixed the boundaries of the peoples*
　　*according to the number of the gods;*

*the Lord's own portion was his people (LXX, laos autou Iakob,
his people Jacob),*

*Jacob his allotted share (LXX, schoinisma kleronomias
autou Israel, Israel was the line of his inheritance).*

In Genesis, Jacob called his sons, and gave his testament (49:2):

*Assemble and hear, O sons of Jacob,
    listen to Israel your father.*

After his testament to Reuben, "my first-born . . . " (Genesis
49:3–4), Jacob said (5–7),

*Simeon and Levi are brothers;
weapons of violence are their swords. . . .
Cursed be their anger, for it is fierce,
    and their wrath, for it is cruel!
I will divide them in Jacob,
    and scatter them in Israel.*

While Israel was encamped in front of Mount Sinai, Moses climbed
the mountain to God. The Lord said to Moses (Exodus 19:3–4):

*Thus you shall say to the house of Jacob, and tell the Israelites:
You have seen what I did to the Egyptians, and how I bore you
on eagles' wings and brought you to myself.*

As such, Jesus would transform the kingdom of David into
the kingdom of God, he would rule over the house of Jacob forever. As the kingdom of God, Jesus' kingdom would have no end.

Jesus "will reign over the house of Jacob forever, and of his
kingdom there will be no end" (Luke 1:33). Fulfilling the messianic
hopes of the house of Jacob, the house of Israel (Exodus 19:3), Jesus'
reign would transcend the house of Jacob. His kingdom would be
an eternal kingdom, coinciding with the kingdom of God. Jesus

would transform the kingdom of David and the house of Jacob into the kingdom of God.

Mary was being told that her son would be the Son of the Most High and that her Son would reign in the kingdom of God! How could this be?

---

1. The preposition of *para* with the dative *(theo)* means "with God," "in the presence of God," and "before God."

2. See Edgar W. Conrad, "The Annunciation of Birth and the Birth of the Messiah," *Catholic Biblical Quarterly* 47 (October 1985) 656–663.

3. In Luke 1:26–38 of the Revised Edition of the New Testament (NAB), the angel Gabriel says "Behold" twice (1:31, 36) and Mary once (1:38).

4. See Adele Berlin, *Poetics and Interpretation of Biblical Narrative* (Sheffield: Almond Press, 1983, 62–63, 91–95.

5. In the New Jerusalem Bible (NJB), the angel Gabriel says, "Look!" (1:31) and Mary says, "You see" (1:38)

6. For theories on the conception of the child of Lucretius, the poet and philosopher *(circa* 94 BC–55 BC), and Galen of Pergamon, whose spectacular career rose from gladiator-physician in Asia Minor to court-physician in the Rome of Marcus Aurelius (AD 129–*circa* 199), see Jan Blayney, "Theories of Conception in the Ancient Roman World," *The Family in Ancient Rome, New Perspectives,* ed. Beryl Rawson (Ithaca: Cornell University Press, 1986), 230–236.

7. *Iesous* (Jesus) is the Greek transliteration of the Hebrew name *Yeshuah* (Joshua), a popular abbreviation of *Yehoshuah.* The name was quite popular among Jews in the Hellenistic and early Roman era.

8. For examples, see the changing of names, from Abram to Abraham, and from Simon to Peter: " . . . and God said to him . . . . No longer shall your name be Abram, but your name shall be Abraham; for I have made you the ancestor of a multitude of nations" (Genesis 17:3–5); Jesus "looked at him and said, 'You are Simon the son of John. You are to be called Cephas' (which is translated Peter)" (John 1:42); "Jesus answered him, 'Blessed are you, Simon, son of Jonah! . . . And I tell you, you are Peter (in Greek, *Petros*), and on this rock (in Greek, *petra*) I will build my church, and the gates of Hades will not prevail against it' " (Matthew 16:13–20, esp. vv. 17–18).

9. The Most High (Hebrew, *El-elyon*; Greek, *Theos Hypsistos*) is the name of the high god of the Canaanite pantheon (Genesis 14:18, 19, 20, 22; Numbers 24:16; Deuteronomy 32:8). See Melchizedek's blessing to Abram:
   "And King Melchizedek of Salem brought out bread and wine; he was priest of God Most High. He blessed him and said,
   'Blessed be Abram by God Most High,
   maker of heaven and earth;
        and blessed be God Most High,
        who has delivered your enemies into your hand' " (Genesis 14:18–20).

   The name became to the Israelites God Most High or Lord (Yahweh) Most High, especially in the book of Psalms and the book of Sirach. Luke frequently uses the title "the Most High" (Luke 1:32, 35, 76; 6:35; 8:28; Acts 7:48; 16:17).

10. See Christopher G. Whitsett, "Son of God, Seed of David: Paul's Messianic Exegesis in Romans 1:3–4," *Journal of Biblical Literature*, 119/4 (Winter 2000) 661–681; and S. Legasse, "Fils de David et Fils de Dieu, Note sur Romains 1,3–4," *Nouvelle Revue Theologique*, 1222/4 (Octobre–Decembre 2000) 564–572.

11. The Lord said to Nathan: "Go and tell my servant David: Thus says the Lord: Are you the one to build me a house to live in? I have not lived in a house since the day I brought up the people of Israel from Egypt to this day, but I have been moving about in a tent and a tabernacle. Wherever I have moved among all the people of Israel, did I ever speak a word with any of the tribal leaders of Israel, whom I commanded to shepherd my people Israel, saying, 'Why have you not built me a house of cedar?' " (2 Samuel 7:5–7).

12. In a slightly different form, the announcement given in 2 Samuel 7:12–16 appears in 1 Chronicles 17:11–14. See Hans Wilhelm Hertzberg, *I & II Samuel* (Philadelphia: Westminster, 1964), 286–287; O. A. Piper, "Messiah," *The International Standard Bible Encyclopedia* (Grand Rapids: William A. Eerdmans, 1986), 3:330–338; E. Jenni, "Messiah, Jewish," *The Interpreter's Dictionary of the Bible* (Nashville: Abingdon, 1982), 3:360–365.

13. Psalm 110:1 (LXX, Psalm 109:1).

14. On Luke 20:41–44, see the development in Peter's Pentecost sermon (Acts 2:25–35) and in Paul's proclamation in the synagogue at Antioch of Pisidia (Acts 13:22–23).

15. For Jesus at the right hand of God, see Acts 2:25; 5:31; 7:55–56; Ephesians 1:20; Colossians 3:1; Hebrews 1:3, 13; 10:12; 1 Peter 3:22.

# Mary's Question

*Mary said to the angel,*
*"How can this be,*
*since I am a virgin?"*
*(Luke 1:34)*

The angel Gabriel had just completed the announcement. How would Mary respond? Not that there was any doubt, not for Mary, even as a virgin.

Mary was fully graced! The Lord was with her! That is how the angel Gabriel greeted her (Luke 1:28):

> *"Greetings* (chaire, *hail*), *favored one!* (kecharitomene, *fully graced*). *The Lord is with you* (ho kyrios meta sou)."

Mary was greatly troubled at his greeting (1:29). Gabriel responded: "Do not be afraid, Mary, for you have found favor (*charis,* grace) with God" (1:30). She was surely in the presence of God.

The angel Gabriel had described Mary's son in messianic terms. Mary would conceive in her womb and bear a son to whom she would give the name Jesus. Her son, Jesus, would be great. He would be called the Son of the Most High. The Lord God would give him the throne of his ancestor David. He would reign over the house of Jacob forever, and of his kingdom there would be no end (1:31–33).

Still, Mary had a question: "How can this be, since I am a virgin?" (1:34).

Ambrose (*circa* 339–397), bishop of Milan (374–397), wrote on Luke 1:34–35:

> *Here Mary seems to have disbelieved, unless you pay close attention, for it is not right that she who was chosen to bear the only-begotten Son of God should seem to have been without faith. And how could this be? Although the prerogative is straightway to be conferred, is intact, how could it be that Zechariah who had not believed was condemned to silence, but Mary, if she had not believed, would be exalted by the infusion of the Holy Spirit? But with a greater prerogative, also a greater faith must be reserved for her.*

But Mary must both believe, and not so heedlessly usurp. She must believe the angel and not usurp divine things. Nor is is easy to know "the mystery which has been hidden from eternity in God" (Ephesians 3:9), which the higher powers could not know either. Nevertheless she did not deny the faith, she did not refuse the duty, but she conformed her will, she promised obedience. For truly when she said, "How shall this be?" she did not doubt concerning the outcome but sought the nature of this same outcome.[1]

In Mary's position, we too would have asked, "How can this be?" We also would invite Gabriel to elaborate his announcement further.

Gabriel had just told Mary that she would be the mother of the Son of the Most High, that her son would be the Son of God in an absolutely unprecedented way, and that her son would reign eternally in the kingdom of God.

After such an announcement (1:31–33), there had to be a question: "How can this be?" But, for whose benefit was this question? Did Mary ask the question on her own behalf, or on ours, Luke's readers, past, present, and future?

## Mary Said to the Angel (1:34a)

From the beginning of the story, "in the sixth month," we have been with Mary. We were there, in the city of Galilee called Nazareth, when Gabriel came and greeted her, when Mary reacted with fear, when she pondered what the greeting meant, and when Gabriel reassured her. With her, we also heard Gabriel's extraordinary announcement.

We may not have noticed, however, that, until now, Mary has not spoken. This is the first time in the story (1:26–38) that Mary actually speaks (1:34).

Mary responded to Gabriel's announcement with a seemingly simple question. But what was Mary really asking? Gabriel's greeting had led Mary to ponder. Mary's question also required pondering, perhaps not on Gabriel's part. Gabriel is among those who stand in the presence of God. God's high-placed emissaries have no need to ponder. We may not be greatly troubled at Mary's question, but we do wonder and ponder what sort of question this might be.

## "How Can This Be, Since I Am a Virgin?" (1:34bc)

There is no getting into Mary's mind. We do not know what Mary, as a historical figure, actually thought. It would be wonderful if we did.[2]

For that matter, we do not even know how Mary actually addressed Gabriel. As an angel, Gabriel did not need human words to communicate with Mary. Nor did Mary need human words to respond. Communicating with an angel, like communicating with God, is very different from ordinary human communication.

For the announcement of the birth of John the Baptist, the angel of the Lord, later to be identified as Gabriel (1:19), appeared (*ophthe*) to Zechariah (1:11). In the Septuagint, the ancient Greek translation of the Old Testament, the Greek term, *ophthe*, "appeared," is used exclusively when God (the Lord), the angel of the Lord, and the glory of God (the Lord) appear. A more literal translation for *ophthe* would be "he made himself to be seen."[3]

Like the appearance of God and the glory of God, the appearance of the angel of the Lord defies description and cannot be adequately portrayed. What is true of Gabriel's appearance is also true of Gabriel's words. Just as Zechariah did not see and hear Gabriel with the ordinary senses, neither did Mary.

We may not know, therefore, precisely what happened historically at the Annunciation. What we can know is how Luke presented Mary as a personage in the story of the Annunciation.[4] For this, we must analyze the role of Gabriel and Mary in the story, how they speak and respond to one another within the Gospel narrative.

In this analysis, we must distinguish between the point of view of Mary and Gabriel as personages in the story and the point of view of the storyteller. For the point of view of Mary as the personage asking the question, we must pay close attention to the immediate context.[5] From the storyteller's point of view, we must pay attention to both the immediate context in the story of the Annunciation and the greater context in the Gospel.

Keeping the two points of view in mind, we begin with the very nature of the question, focusing primarily on the first part, "How can this be?" (1:34a). Again keeping the two points of view in mind, we shall then inquire into the object of Mary's question, this time focusing on each part in turn, "How can this be?" (1:34b) and "Since I am a virgin?" (1:34c).

## The Nature of the Question:
## "How Can This Be?" (1:34b)

A question can mean many things. What precisely is the nature of Mary's question?

In itself, Mary's question, "How can this be, since I am a virgin?" could express disbelief, objecting to Gabriel's message as impossible and having rejection on Mary's part. The question could also be an expression of amazement, a rhetorical question akin to an exclamation, or a joyous request inviting Gabriel to go on and continue the extraordinary announcement.

In other words, Mary's question might imply either a "No!" or a "Yes!" With an implied "No!" Mary's question would be "No! How can this be? This is impossible!" With an implied "Yes!" Mary's question would be "Yes! How can this be? Could anything be so wonderful!"

Of course, the question could also be a simple request for information, neither rejecting nor accepting, just a question, plain and simple, without rhetorical undertones or overtones.

The nature of the question depends on the context. For the nature of Mary's question, we turn to the point of view of the storyteller and the greater context, which includes the question Zechariah asked when Gabriel announced that his wife Elizabeth would bear him a son (1:13–17). The two questions are fairly parallel.

*Zechariah asked,*
    *"How* (kata ti) *will I know* (gnosomai) *that this is so?*
    *For* (gar) *I am an old man, and my wife is getting on in years." (1:18)*

*Mary asked,*
    *"How* (pos) *can this be* (estai),
        *since* (epei) *I am a virgin?" (1:34)*

The questions may be parallel, but their wording is very different. Unfortunately, the difference is somewhat veiled in the English translation; not, however, in the Greek text.

In asking, "How shall I know this?" Zechariah was challenging Gabriel. Zechariah wanted some kind of proof. He asked, "How," that is, "On what basis (*kata ti*) shall I know (*gnosomai*) this?"

In asking, "How can this be?" Mary was not objecting to the announcement. Nor was she asking for proof. She was simply asking how (*pos*) Gabriel's announcement would be (*estai*) fulfilled.

The difference between the two questions can also be seen from Gabriel's responses to Zechariah and Mary. Zechariah had rejected the good news (*euaggelisasthai*) Gabriel brought him (1:19). Because he did not believe Gabriel's words, he would remain speechless and be unable to talk until the day these things took place (1:20). Since he did not believe the good news of John's birth, he would not be able to announce it before John was actually born. To proclaim the good news, one must first have heard it!

By contrast, Gabriel received Mary's question positively. After the angel departed, she would visit her relative Elizabeth. Elizabeth would greet her: "And blessed (*makaria*)[6] is she who believed that there would be a fulfillment of what was spoken to her by the Lord" (1:45). Responding, she then sang of the greatness of the Lord in an outpouring of praise (1:46–55). Having believed in the good news of Jesus' birth, she was able to announce it before the birth of her child.

From the storyteller's point of view, therefore, Mary's question was not an expression of disbelief. Nor was it an objection. Even less a rejection. It was closer to a rhetorical question, an expression of amazement from one who had no relations with a man, inviting the angel to continue with the announcement, as indeed Gabriel would do (1:35–37).

We now turn to the object of Mary's question. For this we must pay close attention to Mary's point of view as presented in the immediate context.

# The Object of Mary's Question:
## "How Can This Be?" (1:34b)

Up to this point, we have reflected on the nature of Mary's question, comparing and contrasting it with Zechariah's question. For this, we focused on the word "how," in Greek, *kata ti*, in the case of Zechariah, and *pos*, in the case of Mary, and the word's implications in each case.

We pointed out that, unlike Zechariah's, Mary's question implied no disbelief. Nor was it an objection, still less a rejection. Unlike Zechariah, Mary did not ask for proof as a condition for accepting the announcement. Mary's question had to do with the reality itself, with how the announcement would be realized.

But what precisely was Mary asking? It may seem obvious: Mary was asking how she could conceive a child while remaining a virgin. But is that really the point of Mary's question? In this, we may be distracted by the polemic and apologetic over Mary's virginity. On further reflection, there may be more to Mary's question than meets the ear.

Our tendency as the readers is to move quickly beyond the first part of the question, "how can this be," to the second part, "since I am a virgin." Doing so, we then interpret the first part in relation to the second, and the question becomes, "How could Mary conceive a child virginally, that is, without having relations with a man?" With that question in mind, we then speak of "the virgin birth" or "the virginal conception."

For many people, the question seems strange. Since Mary was already betrothed to a man named Joseph, she should have known how she would conceive in her womb. This observation, however, presupposes that Mary was asking how she could conceive a child, any child, virginally. Indeed, this is the way Mary's question is understood by a great many interpreters.

If that were the object of Mary's question, it would certainly be puzzling, leading many, especially in the Catholic tradition, to conclude that Mary had made a promise or vow to remain a virgin. Such a vow, however, would lead to another puzzle. Why then was Mary betrothed to Joseph? Normally, a young woman is betrothed in view of eventually living with her husband, having children, raising a family, contributing to the people of God, and ensuring the woman and her husband an enduring place in history.

There is a wide range of interpretations. Paying close attention to the story's narrative logic, some conclude that Mary would become a victim of rape. Others speak of her son's illegitimacy, still others of a conception by Joseph.[7] Some seek a precedent in Greek mythology or in the mythologies of the Ancient Near East. And some speak of Mary conceiving miraculously.[8]

Every one of these interpretations views Mary's virginity as a problem and tries either to solve it or to get around it. All of them also assume that Mary's question was primarily about her virginity.[9]

I believe there may be something wrong with that assumption, and that Mary's virginity is not a good starting point for understanding her question. Literarily, however, the second point, "since I am a virgin" (1:34c), depends on the first, "how can this be" (1:34b). It should be interpreted in relation to the first. The question then becomes, "Without my having relations with a man, how can this be?" That is, "how can this be" concerns a son who shall be the son of the Most High.

Suppose we were to focus initially on the first part of Mary's question, "how can this be," and only then turn to the second part, "since I am a virgin (since I have no relations with a man)." With this starting point, Mary's question would not be primarily about her virginity but about the son she would bear.

Starting with "since I am a virgin (I have no relations with a man)," as we tend to read the question, Mary's son Jesus is seen in relation to Mary's virginity. Starting with "how can this be," as Mary does in the story, Mary's virginity is seen in relation to her son Jesus. Indeed, that is how theological tradition has presented it. Mary's virginity, like her motherhood, is relative to her son, Jesus, not vice versa.

Hearing Mary ask, "How can this be?" our question must be, "How can what be?" The answer to our question lies in Gabriel's previous announcement. How can Mary conceive and bear a son who would be called Son of the Most High?

Mary was asking, "How can I be the mother of the Son of God? How can I be the mother of one who will transform the throne of David into the throne of God's beloved Son? How can I be the mother of one who will reign in the kingdom of God? I am only a virgin! How can a mere virgin, one who is not yet a mother, conceive and bear the Son of the Most High?"

## "Since I Am a Virgin?" (1:34c)

As the story opened, we learned that Elizabeth, in her old age, was in her sixth month. When the angel Gabriel was sent by God to Mary, Mary was still a virgin, albeit "engaged (betrothed) to a man whose name was Joseph, of the house of David" (1:27a). Placing great emphasis on Mary's virginity, the story referred to her virginity a second time while introducing her name: "The virgin's name was Mary" (1:27b).

From this point on, it becomes very clear that the story is about a virgin who will conceive (1:26–33). Only with the second part of Mary's question, "since I am a virgin (since I have no relations with a man)" (1:34c), Gabriel's reply (1:35–37) and Mary's response (1:38), does it become clear that the story is about a virgin who will conceive virginally, that is, without having "relations with a man."

A more literal translation of the Greek for the phrase "since I have no relations with a man" would be "since (*epei*) I do not know (*ou ginosko*) man (*andra*)." The Greek term, "*andra*, man" is a husband. In this context, "knowing" or "not knowing a man" is a semitism for "having" or "not having relations with a man."[10]

For one example, *ginosko* is the word used in the Septuagint:

> *They rose early in the morning and worshiped before the Lord; then they went back* (eiselthen Helkana, *Helkana went*) *to their house* (eis ton oikon autou) *at Ramah* (Armathaim). *Elkanah knew* (egno) *his wife Hannah*[11] (ten Annan gynaika autou), *and the Lord remembered her. In due time Hannah conceived and bore a son. She named him Samuel, for she said, "I have asked him of the Lord." (Hebrew, 1 Samuel 1:19–20; LXX, 1 Kings 1:19–20)*

Paul wrote in his letter to the Galatians that Christ Jesus was "born of a woman," born not with a man:

> *But when the fullness of time had come, God sent his Son, born of a woman* (genomenon ek gynaikos), *born under the law, in order to redeem those who were under the law, so that we might receive adoption as children. (Galatians 4:4–5)*

Mark never mentioned the name of Joseph, but the name of Mary. On the Sabbath, Jesus taught in the synagogue of Nazareth.

> *The people said,*
> *"Where did this man get all this? What is this wisdom that has been given to him? What deeds of power are being done by his hands! Is not this the carpenter, the son of Mary and brother of James and Joses and Judas and Simon, and are not his sisters here with us?" (Mark 6:2–3)*[12]

Luke wrote in his Gospel, "Jesus was about thirty years old when he began his work. He was the son (as was thought, *hos enomizeto*) of Joseph son of Heli" (3:23). In Luke, Joseph was not the father of Jesus. In his prologue, we read in the story of the child in the temple (2:41–52):

> *When his parents saw him they were astonished; and his mother said to him, "Child, why have you treated us like this? Your father and I have been searching for you in great anxiety." He said to them, "Why were you searching for me? Did you not know that I must be in my Father's house?" (2:48–49)*

Mary, his mother, said to Jesus, "your father," which later came to be understood as "your foster-father."[13]

In the Annunciation, Mary's question to the angel presupposes that she does not foresee "knowing" or having relations with a man at least in the immediate future, even though she is betrothed to Joseph.

Mary's basic question to the angel was, "How can I possibly be the mother of one who is called the Son of the Most High, of one who will reign over the house of Jacob (Israel) forever, of one who will rule over the kingdom of God? How can this be?"

The second part of the question can be interpreted eliptically to say, "since (*epei*) I am a virgin (since I have no relations with a man)" (1:34c). The Greek term *epei*, which is usually given a causal sense and translated as "since," thus retains its causal meaning but in the sense of "besides," "then," or "morever." Mary's not having relations with a man buttresses her basic question, "How can this be?" (1:34b). It is also the introduction to the angel's reply: "The Holy Spirit will come upon you, and the power of the Most High will overshadow you" (1:35a).

Not having relations with a man is a secondary concern. The primary concern is the human conception of the Son of God.

In Luke's story of the Annunciation, Mary is clearly presented as a virgin (*parthenos*), and her question, "How can this be?" asks how she can be the mother of the Son of the Most High. Were

Mary to conceive an ordinary child, however great, having no relations with a man would be an obstacle and seen as a problem. For conceiving the Son of the Most High, however, conceiving virginally is no obstacle. It can actually be seen as a solution.

Conceiving and bringing forth the Son of the Most High has nothing to do with having relations with a man. No human relationship, no human effort, would enable Mary to conceive the Son of God. Divine life is not spun from human stuff. It can only come from God.

1.  Saint Ambrose of Milan, *Exposition of the Holy Gospel According to Saint Luke with Fragments on the Prophecy of Isaias*, trans. T. Tomkinson (Etna, California: Center for Traditionalist Orthodox Studies, 1998), 40.

2.  For a critique of "psychological explanations" concerning the logic of Mary's question in 1:34, see Raymond E. Brown, ss, *The Birth of the Messiah* (New York: Doubleday, 1993), 303–307.

3.  See above, "Setting and Personages," pp. 40–41.

4.  For a "literary explanation" concerning the logic of Mary's question in 1:34, see Brown, *The Birth of the Messiah*, 307–309.

5.  In "Narrative Logic in the Annunciation to Mary (Luke 1:26–38)," *Journal of Biblical Literature,* 114 (1995) 65–79, David T. Landry distinguishes between explanations based on "the psychology of the historical Mary," and the psychology of Mary as a character in the narrative (see especially 70). In the same way, we may discuss the psychology of Hamlet in Shakespeare's play quite apart from the psychology of the historical prince of Denmark. Landry's distinction is very helpful, inviting us to distinguish between two kinds of literary explanation, one paying attention to the point of view of the author or narrator, the other paying attention to the point of view of Mary, a personage in the narrative.

6.  See Luke 11:27–28, "While he was saying this, a woman in the crowd raised her voice and said to him, 'Blessed (*makaria*) is the womb that bore you and the breasts that nursed you!' But he said, 'Blessed (*makarioi*) rather are those who hear the word of God and obey it.'" The words "*makarios, makaria* (blessed), are in the four beatitudes (*makarioi*) of Luke's "Sermon on the Plain" (6:20–23): "Blessed (*makarioi*) are you who are poor, for yours is the kingdom of God" (6:20); the nine beatitudes (*makarioi*) of Matthew's "Sermon on the

Mount" (Matthew 5:1–12): "Blessed (*makarioi*) are the poor in spirit, for theirs is the kingdom of heaven" (5:3).

7. See Jane Shaberg, *The Illegitimacy of Jesus: A Feminist Theological Interpretation of the Infancy Narratives* (San Francisco: Harper and Row, 1987). For an incisive critique, see David Landry, "Narrative Logic in the Annunciation to Mary (Luke 1:26–38)," 68–79. For a response to the charge of illegitimacy in general, see Brown, *The Birth of the Messiah*, Appendix V, 534–542.

8. Concerning the virginal conception and its place in the development of tradition, see Brown, *The Birth of the Messiah*, Appendix IV, 517–533.

9. All of these, including Shaberg, assume that since Mary is the personage addressed by Gabriel, Mary is also the principal subject of the story.

10. "The verb *ginoskein* is used euphemistically of marital relations, a usage well attested in Hellenistic Greek and in the LXX (e.g. Judg 11:39; 21:12; Gen 19:8)." Joseph A. Fitzmyer, SJ, *The Gospel According to Luke I–IX*, Anchor Bible 28 (New York: Doubleday, 1981), 384, n. 34.

11. In Hebrew, the name was Hannah. In Greek, it was *Anna*, which translated into English is Ann. Hannah's hymn of praise (1 Samuel 2:1–10) inspired Mary's hymn of praise, the Magnificat. It was a little step to relate the mother of Samuel to the mother of Jesus. Hannah, *Anna,* Ann, was the spiritual mother of Mary.

12. See Mark 3:31–35, "Then his mother and his brothers came; and standing outside, they sent to him and called him. A crowd was sitting around him; and they said to him, 'Your mother and your brothers and sisters are outside, asking for you.' And he replied, 'Who are my mother and my brothers?' And looking at those who sat around him, he said, 'Here are my mother and my brothers! Whoever does the will of God is my brother and sister and mother.'"

13. "The expression 'his parents' (*hoi goneis autou*, vv. 41, 43) now becomes more explicit, 'your father and I.' One should not immediately think that Mary means 'your foster-father.' "Fitzmyer, *The Gospel According to Luke I–IX*, Anchor Bible 28 (New York: Doubleday, 1981), 443, n. 2:48.

# The Angel's Answer to Mary

*The angel said to her,*
*"The Holy Spirit will come upon you,*
*and the power of the Most High*
*will overshadow you;*
*therefore the child to be born*
*will be holy; he will be called Son of God.*
*And now, your relative Elizabeth*
*in her old age has also conceived a son;*
*and this is the sixth month for her*
*who was said to be barren.*
*For nothing will be impossible with God."*
*(Luke 1:35–37)*

In the story of the Annunciation to Mary, we now enter the third and last phase in the dialogue between the angel Gabriel and the virgin Mary (Luke 1:35–38). The angel Gabriel answered Mary's question (1:35–37) and Mary gave her response to the angel Gabriel (1:38).

In the first phase, the angel Gabriel greeted Mary, "Greetings (*chaire*, hail), favored one (*kecharitomene*, fully graced)! The Lord is with you" (1:28). Gabriel's greeting was much perplexing (very troubling) for Mary and left her pondering what the greeting meant (1:29).

In the second phase, the angel Gabriel responded to Mary's reaction and explained what the greeting meant. Addressing Mary by name, the angel said to her: "Do not be afraid, Mary, for you have found favor (*charis*, grace) with God." Mary was fully graced (*kecharitomene*). Having found grace (*charis*) with God, she had no reason to be afraid (1:30).

Gabriel then announced that Mary would conceive in her womb, bear a son, and name him Jesus. Like David, who was God's adopted son (2 Samuel 7:14), Mary's son would be great and be called the Son of the Most High. The Lord God would give him the throne of his ancestor David, and he would reign over the house of Jacob forever. In Jesus, the kingdom of David would become the kingdom of God (Luke 1:31–33).

Reassured by Gabriel, Mary was no longer troubled. After Gabriel's announcement, she also knew what the greeting was about and some of its implications. But she had a question. How could this be? How could she conceive, bear, and name a son who would be called the Son of the Most High? Mary was just a humble virgin. She had no relations with a man. How could she become the mother of the Son of the Most High (1:34)?

In the third phase, Gabriel answers Mary's question (1:35–37). There was still more to the announcement. To this point, Gabriel had given Mary only the first part, announcing the fact of Jesus' conception and birth together with Jesus' identity as royal Messiah (1:30–33). Prompted by Mary's question (1:34), Gabriel now gives the second part, announcing how Jesus would be conceived and how his conception would give him a unique identity as the Son of God (1:35–37).

The Holy Spirit would come upon Mary (1:35a), and the power of the Most High would overshadow her (1:35b). That is how the one to be born would be called holy, the Son of God (1:35c). David was God's son by adoption. Conceived by the Holy Spirit, Jesus was the Son of God by nature.

Gabriel then concludes the announcement. Mary's relative, Elizabeth, had conceived in her old age and was already in her sixth month. For Mary, this would be a sign that nothing was impossible for God (1:36–37).

Gabriel's reply can be divided into two parts. In the first part, Gabriel answers Mary's question and completes the announcement concerning Jesus' birth. Mary's son would be the Son of God (1:35). In the second part, Gabriel offers Mary a sign, associating the conception of Jesus with the conception of John the Baptist (1:5–25) and the conception of Isaac (Genesis 17:15–22; 18:9–15; 21:1–8). Far more, however, than the conception of John the Baptist and Isaac, the conception of Jesus will transform the whole of salvation history. Indeed, nothing is impossible for God (Luke 1:36–37)!

## "The Holy Spirit Will Come Upon You" (1:35a)

Then, responding (*kai apokritheis*), the angel said to her, "The Holy Spirit will come upon you" (1:35a). Conceiving the Son of the Most High had nothing to do with having relations with a man. For Mary to conceive and give birth to the Son of God, the Holy Spirit, the creative Spirit of God, would come upon her.

This is the second time the Holy Spirit is mentioned in Luke's Gospel.[1] The first mention also came from Gabriel, in the announcement of the birth of John Baptist. Zechariah's prayer had been heard. Elizabeth would bear him a son. "Even (*eti*) before his birth (from his mother's womb, *ek koilias metros autou*) he will be filled with the Holy Spirit" (1:15c). Filled with the Spirit of prophecy, John would go before the Lord "with the spirit and power of Elijah . . . to make ready a people prepared for the Lord" (1:17).

John would be filled with the Holy Spirit from his mother's womb. From his very birth, John would be "the prophet of the Most High" (1:76). Jesus, however, would be conceived by the Holy

Spirit. From his very conception, Jesus would be the Son of the Most High (1:32).

Bearing Jesus' life (1:35, 38), Mary left from the city of Nazareth to the city of Judah to visit her relative Elizabeth, who was bearing John's life in her sixth month: "In those days Mary set out and went with haste to a Judean town (*eis polin*, to a city) in the hill country, where she entered the house of Zechariah and greeted Elizabeth" (1:39–40). As a result of Mary's greeting, John leaped in his mother's womb (1:41). Before his birth, John was quickened, filled with the Holy Spirit (1:15) "to make ready a people prepared for the Lord" (1:17).

Ostensibly, the principal personages in this visitation (1:39–56) are Mary and Elizabeth. In reality, however, the main personages are the unborn infants, Jesus and John.[2] Conceived by the Holy Spirit, Jesus in Mary's womb sent the Holy Spirit to John, who leapt in Elizabeth's womb. In Luke's Gospel, the two meetings are between Jesus and John the Baptist. The first meeting would be this prenatal encounter (1:39–41a) and the second meeting would be at Jesus' baptism (3:21–22).

There is a great difference between the conception and birth of John and the conception and birth of Jesus. The difference can be seen in the role of the Holy Spirit. In the case of John, the Holy Spirit would come not upon Zechariah or Elizabeth but on John himself, who would be filled with the Holy Spirit in his mother's womb. In the case of Jesus, the Holy Spirit would come not on Jesus himself but upon Mary, the mother of Jesus. That is how she would "conceive in your womb and bear a son" (1:31). And that is how Jesus would be the Son of God by nature (1:35c), not just by adoption.

In Luke-Acts, the Holy Spirit is the Spirit of prophecy, as in Elizabeth's greeting to Mary (1:41–45), and in the prophetic canticles of Zechariah (1:67–79) and Simeon (2:25, 29–32), where the Spirit of prophecy is also the Spirit of revelation (2:26). The Holy

Spirit is also the Spirit of mission, as at the beginning of Jesus' ministry. After Jesus was baptized and while he was praying, the heavens opened, the Holy Spirit descended "upon him in bodily form like a dove," and a voice from heaven addressed him: "You are my Son, the Beloved (*agapetos*);[3] with you I am well pleased" (3:21–22).

From his very conception, Jesus was the Son of God (1:26–38). His identity as God's beloved Son was announced to him after he was baptized (3:21–22). Later, it would be revealed to an inner circle of apostles, Peter, James, and John, at his Transfiguration (9:28–36).

To appreciate the uniqueness of Jesus as Son of God, we may compare his conception with that of an ordinary child and with that of a Christian who shares in Jesus' divine life.

For the conception of an ordinary child, a woman must have relations with a man. That is how God intended it to be, creating the human being in the divine image. God, the creator, created the human couple to be co-creators. That is why God created them male and female (Genesis 1:20):

> *So God created humankind in his image,*
> *in the image of God he created them;*
> *male and female he created them.*

That is how it would be for the first man born of woman: "Now the man knew his wife Eve, and she conceived and bore Cain, saying, 'I have produced a man with the help of the Lord'" (4:1). And that is how it would be for all human beings, including David, whom God adopted when David was anointed king.

Jesus would be the one exception. The conception of Jesus, the Son of the Most High, did not depend on the relationship between "male and female" (1:27c) in which a man and a woman "become one flesh" (2:24). God's life, the life of the Son of God, is not spun from human stuff. From the very beginning, Jesus' life came directly from God. Born of a woman, Jesus would be truly human; born of God, he would also be divine (Galatians 4:4–5):

> *But when the fullness of time had come,*
> *God* (ho theos) *sent his Son* (ton huion auton),
> *born of a woman* (genomenon ek gynaikos),
> *born under the law, in order to redeem those who were*
> *under the law, so that we might receive adoption as children.*[4]

Christians, like other children, are conceived by their parents as human beings, not as Christians. It is only later, in Baptism, that they become Christians: "In Christ Jesus you are all children of God through faith" (3:26). Like an ordinary child, a Christian's conception and birth depend on the relationship between "male and female." Becoming children of God, however, does not. As Christians, we are children of God by adoption.

As a human being, a Christian may have been born a Jew or a Greek, a slave, the child of a slave, or a free person, a male child or a female child. But in baptism, everyone, Jew or Greek, slave or free, man or woman, puts on Christ and becomes one in Christ. Everyone, through Baptism, becomes a Christian, irrespective of his or her human background. Becoming adopted children of God has nothing to do with the relationship of "male and female" (3:28).

John's Gospel taught the same thing, but in different terms (1:12–13):

> *But to all who received him* (the Word and the Light),
> *who believed in his name* (eis to onoma autou),
> *he gave power to become children of God* (tekna theou),
> *who were born, not of blood* (ex haimaton)
> *or of the will of flesh* (ek thelematos sarkos)
> *or of the will of man* (ek thelematos andros),
> *but of God.*

As human beings, those who become children of God are conceived by natural generation. As God's children by adoption, however, they are virginally conceived. Born of God, they are born from above of water and Spirit (John 3:3–8).

With Jesus, the Word made flesh, it was different. No human relationship, including the relationship between "male and female," indeed no human effort, including the most spiritual, could have resulted in his conception as the Son of the Most High. There was absolutely nothing Mary could have done, fully graced that she was, to conceive the Son of God.

Fully graced (*kecharitomene*), the Lord was with Mary (Luke 1:28). She had found grace (*charis*) before God (1:30). That made her able to accept the word of God and welcome the Holy Spirit, but did not enable her to conceive the Son of God.

That is why the Holy Spirit would come upon (*epeleusetai*) Mary, as it would come upon the apostles on Pentecost, for the conception and birth of the Church (Acts 1:8; see 2:1–4). In the case of the Church, however, the Holy Spirit came upon the apostles that they might be Jesus' "witnesses in Jerusalem, in all Judea and Samaria, and to the ends of the earth" (1:8). In the case of Jesus, the Holy Spirit came upon Mary that she might conceive the Son of the Most High. Like Jesus' identity as the Son of God, Mary's mission to be the mother of the Son of God was absolutely unique.

## "And the Power of the Most High Will Overshadow You" (1:35b)

After telling Mary that the Holy Spirit would come upon her (1:35a), the angel told her that the power of the Most High would overshadow her. Since Jesus would "be called the Son of the Most High" (1:32a), he would be conceived by "the power of the Most High (*dynamis hypsistou*)." In the Old Testament, God is often referred to as "the Most High," in Hebrew, *'Elyon*, translated in the

Septuagint as *Hypsistos*, a popular title for Zeus throughout the Hellenistic world.

The expression "the power (*dynamis*) of the Most High," like "the power (*dynamis*) of the Lord" (5:17) and "power (*dynamis*) from on high" (24:49), refers to the Holy Spirit. In each case, we see that by comparing the expressions with closely related texts in Luke-Acts.

## The Power of the Lord

In Luke 5:17, the expression "the power of the Lord" recalls the expression "the power of the Spirit," used to introduce and describe all of Jesus' Galilean ministry (4:14–15):

> *Then Jesus, filled with the power of the Spirit* (en te dynamei tou pneumato), *returned to Galilee, and a report about him spread through all the surrounding country. He began to teach in their synagogues and was praised by everyone.*

The phrase to which it belongs, "the power of the Lord (*dynamis kyriou*) was with him to heal" (5:17b), refers back to Jesus' inaugural address in the synagogue at Nazareth (4:18–19), where Jesus summarized his entire mission in the words of Isaiah 61:1–2:

> *The Spirit of the Lord is upon me*
> > *because he has anointed me*
> *to bring good news to the poor.*
> *He has sent me to proclaim release to the captives*
> > *and recovery of sight to the blind,*
> *to let the oppressed go free,*
> *to proclaim the year of the Lord's favor.*

In the synagogue at Nazareth, Jesus announced that the Spirit of the Lord was upon him that he might bring good news to the poor, liberty to captives, sight to the blind, and freedom to the oppressed. The Spirit of the Lord was upon Jesus that he might heal all those who were in need of healing.

The story of Jesus curing a paralytic (5:17–26), like that of the cleansing of a leper (5:12–16), is a good example of Jesus' healing mission. It is for that mission that "the power of the Lord (the power of the Spirit, the Spirit of the Lord) was with him to heal" (5:17).

## Power from on High

In Luke 24:49, the risen Jesus had just told the community: "And see (*idou*, behold) I am sending upon you what my Father promised" (24:49a). He then told them: "so stay here in the city until you have been clothed with power from on high" (24:49b). The expression "power from on high" interprets the previous expression, "the promise of my Father." Later, in the prologue of Acts, Jesus associates the same "power" with the Holy Spirit: "But you will receive power when the Holy Spirit has come upon you" (Acts 1:8). The Holy Spirit would come on Pentecost (2:1–4), empowering the apostles to speak the good news (2:14–41) and to cure those in need (see 3:1–10), just as Jesus had done.

## The Power of the Most High

In the story of the Annunciation, Gabriel's reply is close to Hebrew poetry, where the parallel expressions are used to interpret one another. Here the expression "the power of the Most High" presents the Holy Spirit from the viewpoint of divine power. The phrase "the power of the Most High will overshadow (*episkiasei*) you" (1:35b) parallels the previous phrase, "the Holy Spirit will come upon you" (1:35a). The two expressions "the power of the Most High" and "the Holy Spirit," like the two phrases, interpret one another.

In the phrase "the power of the Most High will overshadow you," the word "overshadow" (*episkiasei*)[5] evokes the presence of God in the form of a cloud upon the Israelite sanctuary or the tabernacle during the Israelite Exodus (Exodus 40:34–38).

*Then the cloud covered the tent of meeting, and the glory of the*
*Lord filled the tabernacle. Moses was not able to enter the tent*
*of meeting because the cloud settled down (LXX, epeskiazen,*
*overshadowed) upon it, and the glory of the Lord filled the*
*tabernacle. Whenever the cloud was taken up from the tabernacle,*
*the Israelites would set out on each stage of their journey; but*
*if the cloud was not taken up, then they did not set out until*
*the day that it was taken up. For the cloud of the Lord was on*
*the tablernacle by day, and fire was in the cloud by night, before*
*the eyes of the house of Israel at each stage of their journey.*

As the power of the Most High will overshadow Mary, the womb
of Mary will be the sanctuary, the tent of meeting, the tabernacle,
and the dwelling place of God.[6]

The word "overshadow" also evokes Jesus' Transfiguration
(Luke 9:28–36). When Jesus took Peter, John and James up the
mountain to pray, Moses and Elijah appeared in glory and spoke of
Jesus' exodus that he would fulfill in Jerusalem. Seeing his glory,
Peter suggested they they make three tents, one for Jesus, one for
Moses, and one for Elijah. While Peter was still speaking "a cloud
came and overshadowed (*epeskiazen*) them" (9:34).[7]

## "Therefore the Child to Be Born Will Be Holy; He Will Be Called Son of God" (1:35c).

While Jesus was praying after his Baptism, the Holy Spirit would
descend upon him and a voice from heaven would address him:
"You are my Son, the Beloved (*ho agapetos*); with you I am well
pleased" (3:21–22). Then, while Jesus was praying on the mountain
and was transfigured, Moses and Elijah would appear in glory and a
voice from the cloud would address Peter, John, and James: "This is
my Son, my Chosen (*ho eklelegmenos*); listen to him" (9:35). Both
events are very important regarding Jesus' identity.

Gabriel's statement in the Annunciation, however, is even more basic: "Therefore the child to be born will be holy; he will be called Son of God" (1:35c).

At the Annunciation, Gabriel announced to Mary that the Holy Spirit would come upon her (1:35a), and the power of the Most High would overshadow her (1:35b), and for this reason the child would be holy and would be called Son of God (1:35c). Predicated of Jesus, the adjective "holy" and the title "Son of God" parallel the adjective "great" and the title "Son of the Most High," applied to Jesus earlier in Gabriel's announcement (1:32). To appreciate Jesus' identity as "holy" and the "Son of God" in the context of Gabriel's reply (1:35), we must see it in relation to Mary's question (1:34).

Together, Mary's question and Gabriel's reply are in the form of a chiasm, whose structure can be represented as A B B' A', where the first part of Mary's question (A) corresponds to the second part of Gabriel's response (A'), and the second part of Mary's question (B) corresponds to the first part of Gabriel's response (B'). Theoretically, the chiasm may seem complicated, but rhetorically, the chiasm describes a very natural pattern. Here is the pattern for Mary's question and Gabriel's reply.

Mary's question:

(A) "How can this be (1:34a),

(B) since I am a virgin (I do not know man; I have no relations with a man)" (1:34b)?

Gabriel's reply:

(B') "The Holy Spirit will come upon you, and the power of the Most High will overshadow you (1:35a);

(A') therefore, the child to be born will be holy; he will be called Son of God" (1:35b).

Mary's basic question is (A), "How can this be?" As the part of her question, she then gives the reason for raising it (B), "since I am a virgin (I do not know man; I have no relations with a man)."

Gabriel begins by responding (B') to the reason why Mary raised the question (B). The announcement, "The Holy Spirit will come upon you, and the power of the Most High will overshadow you" (B') responds to what Mary sees as an obstacle (B), "Since I am a virgin (I do not know man; I have no relations with a man)."

Only then does Gabriel respond (A') to the basic question itself (A). The announcement, "Therefore, the child to be born will be holy: he will be called Son of God" (A') responds to Mary's basic question (A), "How can this be?" How can I be the mother of the Son of the Most High?

Gabriel's introductory word (A',1:35b), "therefore" (*dio kai*) carries a causal[8] as well as a logical connotation, for which I suggest the translation, "And that is how." Mary asked, "How can this be" (A, 1:34a). Gabriel answers, "And that is how," that is, that is how you will conceive in your womb and bear a son who will be called the Son of the Most High (1:31–32): "The Holy Spirit will come upon you, and the power of the Most High will overshadow you." Conceived by the Holy Spirit, Jesus will be holy and the Son of God by nature, not just great and the Son of God by adoption.

## "And Now, Your Relative Elizabeth in Her Old Age Has Also Conceived a Son; and This Is the Sixth Month for Her Who Was Said to Be Barren" (1:36)

The story of the Annunciation to Mary began with a reference to the story of the annunciation to Zechariah, "In the sixth month" (1:26). With that simple temporal indication, "In the sixth month," Luke recalls how, after Zechariah's wife Elizabeth conceived, "for five months she remained in seclusion. She said, 'This is what the Lord has done for me and took away the disgrace I have endured among my people'" (1:24–25). Now it was the sixth month, and Elizabeth was no longer in seclusion. What the Lord had done for her could now be announced.

After responding to Mary's question, "How can this be, since I am a virgin (I do not know man; I have no relations with a man)?" (1:34), Gabriel tells Mary about Elizabeth and how she conceived in her old age. In the announcement, Gabriel also refers to "the sixth month (*to meni to ekto*)" (see 1:26), describing what was so significant about it: "And now (*idou*, behold), your relative Elizabeth in her old age has also conceived a son; and this is the sixth month (*men ektos*) for her who was said to be barren" (1:36).

At the beginning of the story, the narrator's reference to the sixth month connected the Annunciation of Jesus' conception and birth (1:26–38) to that of John the Baptist (1:5–25), suggesting that the life and mission of Jesus should be seen in relation to the life and mission of John the Baptist. Toward the end of the story, Gabriel concludes the announcement to Mary by relating John's conception and birth to the conception and birth of Jesus, now suggesting that the conception of John prepared the way for the conception of Jesus.

Elizabeth is described as Mary's relative or kinswoman (*he syggenis*) without further specification. Popularly, many refer to Elizabeth as Mary's cousin. This focuses attention on the blood relationship between Mary and Elizabeth and indirectly on the family relationship between Jesus and John. The term "relative" is much broader. According to the Gospel of John, John the Baptist did not know Jesus personally (John 1:31, 33), and the relationship indicated may have had nothing to do with Jesus' family.

Instead, the relationship between Mary and Elizabeth may be historical and theological. Elizabeth's conception of John in her old age prepared the way for Mary's conception of Jesus as a virgin, just as John the Baptist would prepare the way for the mission of Jesus. Mary and Elizabeth, like Jesus and John, may not have been related by blood. But they were surely related theologically in the history of salvation.

## "For Nothing Will Be Impossible with God" (1:37)

That Elizabeth conceived in her old age and was now in her sixth month, ready for the child to be quickened in his mother's womb (see 1:41), is offered to Mary as a sign that "nothing will be impossible (*ouk adynatesei . . . pan hrema*)" for God (1:37). The Greek expression here translated as "nothing" is *ouk . . . pan hrema*, literally, "not every word."

In Greek, there are two words, *logos* and *hrema*, that are translated as our English term, "word." One of those words, *logos*, is quite well known, even by people unfamiliar with the Greek language. This is the word we find in the prologue of John's Gospel: "In the beginning was the Word (*ho logos*), and the Word (*ho logos*) was with God, and the Word (*ho logos*) was God" (John 1:1). For another example, in Luke's Gospel, *logos* is the word Jesus used when he told the crowd: "My mother and my brothers are those who (*houtoi*) hear (*eisin akouontes*) the word of God (*ton logon tou theou*) and do it" (8:21). The other word, *hrema*, is unfamiliar to most people.

In the Septuagint, *hrema* is used to translate the Hebrew word *dabar*, and from there it passed into the New Testament where it appears quite frequently. For example, *hrema* is the word Peter used when he told Jesus, "Master, we have worked all night long but have caught nothing. Yet if you say so (*epi de to hremati sou*, on your word), I will let down the nets" (5:5).

In the New Testament, as in the Sepuagint, the term *hrema* refers to a "word" in relation to the reality it conveys. That is why it can also be translated as "thing," as in "*nothing* will be impossible with God." On the other hand, the term *logos* refers to a "word" in relation to the idea or the message it conveys. While the term *hrema* denotes the reality conveyed by a word, the term *logos* denotes the idea contained in a word.

The phrase, "nothing will be impossible with God," literally, "with God every word will not be impossible," evokes the Lord's word to Abraham: "Shall anything be impossible with God (*me ady-natesei para to theo rema*, LXX, Genesis 18:14).[9] Like Elizabeth, Sarah, Abraham's wife, had been barren until she conceived a son in her old age. Addressed to Mary, *hrema* (word, thing) refers to her conceiving the Son of God through the power of the Holy Spirit. As in the case of Sarah and Elizabeth, "nothing will be impossible with God."

---

1. The term "Holy Spirit (*Pneuma hagion*)" is used 17 times in Luke's Gospel (1:15, 35, 41, 67; 2:25, 26, 27; 3:16, 22; 4:1 (twice), 14, 18; 10:21; 11:13; 12:10, 12); in the Acts of the Apostles, it appears in 1:2, 5, 8, 16; 2:4 (twice), 33, 38; 4:8, 25, 31; 5:3, 9, 32.

2. For the Visitation (Luke 1:39–56), see E. LaVerdiere, *Luke*, New Testament Message 5 (Collegeville: The Liturgical Press, 1980, 1990) 20–23: " . . . their mothers' primary function was to articulate the significance of their pre-natal encounter," 22.

3. See Genesis 22:2 in the Hebrew, "Then God said: 'Take your son Isaac, your only one, whom you love, and go to the land of Moriah. There you shall offer him up as a holocaust on a height that I will point out to you.'" See the same verse in the Septuagint: "And he (God) said, 'Take your son, the beloved (*ton agapeton*), whom you love—Isaac, and go into the high land, and offer him there as a holocaust on one of the mountains which I will tell you.'" Later, Genesis 22:12, 16, in the Hebrew and the Septuagint, we will read "the beloved (*ho agapetos*)."

4. For the term, "adoption as children (*huiothesia*)," see Frank J. Matera, *Galatians*, Sacra Pagina 9 (Collegeville: The Liturgical Press, 1992) 150–151, n. Gal. 1:5, "*Hyiosthesia* was the legal term for adoption in the Greco-Roman world;" see also *huiothesia*, *Theological Dictionary of the New Testament* (Grand Rapids: Eerdmans Company, 1972), Peter Wulfing von Martitz, 1. In the Greek World, 8:397–398; Eduard Schweizer, 2. In Judaism, and 3. In the New Testament 8:399. In the New Testament, the word *huiothesia* only occurs in the Pauline letters (Romans 8:15, 23; 9:4; Galatians 4:5; Ephesians 1:5).

5. See Psalm 91:4 (LXX, Psalm 90:4), "he will cover (*episkiasei*, overshadow) you with his pinions, and under his wings you will find refuge; his faithfulness is a shield and buckler."

6. John J. Kilgallen, "The Conception of Jesus (Luke 1,35)," *Biblica* 78 (1997) 225–246; see pp. 229–230.

7. See Acts 5:15–16, "so that they even carried out the sick into the streets, and laid them on cots and mats, in order that Peter's shadow (*skia*) might fall (*episkiase*, overshadow) on some of them as he came by. A great number of people would also gather from the towns around Jerusalem, bringing the sick and those tormented by unclean spirits, and they were all cured."

8. For Luke's use of *dio* in a causal sense, see Raymond E. Brown, SS, *The Birth of the Messiah* (New York: Doubleday, 1993), 291, and Joseph A. Fitzmyer, SJ, *The Gospel According to Luke I–IX*, Anchor Bible 28 (New York: Doubleday, 1981), 351.

9. See also Job 42:2 and Zechariah 8:6.

# Mary's Response

*Then Mary said,*
*"Here I am,*
*the servant of the Lord;*
*let it be with me*
*according to your word."*
*Then the angel departed from her.*
*(Luke 1:38)*

The angel Gabriel had just announced to Mary that the Holy Spirit would come upon her and the power of the Most High would overshadow her, and her child to be born would be holy; he would be called Son of God (Luke 1:35). Nothing is impossible with God!

The story of the Annunciation to Mary now concludes with Mary's response and the departure of the angel Gabriel (1:38). From the very beginning, with Gabriel's first greeting to Mary (1:28), even before the announcement (1:30–33), we knew how Mary would respond. We now hear it from her.

In every language, many people speak of Mary's response as her *fiat*, her *fiat* to Gabriel's announcement, her *fiat* to the coming of the Holy Spirit, her *fiat* to conceive a son, whom she would name Jesus, her *fiat* to the incarnation and all that it implies.

*Fiat* is the Latin word for "Let it be" (New Revised Standard Version), "May it be done" (Revised New Testament of New American Bible and New American Standard Bible), "Let it happen"

(New Jerusalem Bible), or "So be it" (The New English Bible); that is, "Let it be with me according to your word."

After Gabriel announced that Mary would conceive and bear the Son of the Most High (1:31–33), Mary asked, "How can this be, since I am a virgin (*epei andra ou ginosko*, since I do not know man; since I have no relations with a man)?" (1:34).

Answering, Gabriel continued the announcement (1:35–37), telling Mary how she would conceive. The Holy Spirit would come upon her and the power of the Most High would overshadow her. That is why "the child to be born will be holy; he will be called Son of God" (1:35b). Concluding, the angel gave Mary a sign. Her relative Elizabeth had also conceived in her old age. She who was called barren was in the sixth month, "For nothing will be impossible with God" (1:37).

Mary's question (1:34) was answered (1:35–37)! Conceiving and bearing the Son of the Most High had nothing to do with having sexual relations with a man. For an ordinary child, relations with a man were necessary, but not for the Son of the Most High. The Holy Spirit would come upon her. To conceive the Son of the Most High, the power of the Most High, the creative Spirit of God, would overshadow her.

If this were an ordinary biblical annunciation of a birth, the story could end here, noting only Gabriel's departure. Sent from God to a virgin engaged (betrothed) to a man whose name was Joseph, the angel Gabriel would have completed his mission.

In the story of the annunciation to Zechariah, Gabriel did not need Zechariah's response. The angel Gabriel replied to Zechariah (1:19–20):

> *I am Gabriel. I stand in the presence of God, and I have been sent to speak to you and to bring you this good news. But now, because you did not believe my words, which will be fulfilled in their time, you will become mute, unable to speak, until the day these things occur.*

Among biblical stories announcing a birth, the Annunciation to Mary is unique. In relation to the birth of Jesus, the Son of the Most High, the story is an annunciation story. But in relation to Mary, who would conceive and bring him forth, it is also a commission story, inviting Mary to become the mother of Jesus, the Son of the Most High.

Having completed the announcement, Gabriel's mission from God was not yet over. Before departing, Gabriel had to receive Mary's response. Her response came with no hesitation (1:38).

We may reflect on Mary's response as a critical moment in the history of salvation. The Incarnation depended on it, and without it there would have been no redemption. The story of grace is both divine and human.

But we should not dramatize the moment, as though the salvation of the world were in precarious balance and Gabriel was anxiously awaiting Mary's response. Mary responded very simply, as one who hears the word of God and does it (8:21), *a fortiori*, as one who has found grace (*charin*) with God (1:30).

Like every part, indeed every word, in the story of the Annunciation, Mary's response is filled with biblical resonance. After hearing the rest of the story, we expect the response to be great, and we are not disappointed. As the angel Gabriel departs from her, we are left contemplating her *fiat* and pondering its challenge.

Mary's *fiat* responded to everything the angel had said to her, beginning with the greeting, "Greetings (*chaire*, hail), favored one (*kecharitomene*, fully graced one, wondrously graced one)! The Lord is with you (*ho kyrios meta sou*)" (1:28), and ending with the announcement that Elizabeth was in the sixth month, showing that "nothing will be impossible with God" (1:37).

The response came in two parts:

*"Here I am, the servant of the Lord" (1:38a)*; and
*"let it be with me according to your word" (1:38b)*.

The first part refers to Mary's personal relationship to the Lord. The second part refers to her fulfillment of what the angel announced to her.

The two parts of Mary's response are closely related. To understand the first, we have to understand the second, and vice versa. It was as "the servant of the Lord" that Mary spoke her *fiat* ("let it be with me according to your word") and her *fiat* ("let it be with me according to your word") showed what it meant for her to be "the servant of the Lord."

It was the same with the angel's greeting and the announcement. To understand the greeting, we had to understand the announcement, and vice versa. Mary was fully and wondrously graced, and the Lord was already with her (1:28). But now, the Lord would be with her in an even more extraordinary way (1:30–33, 35). Mary was graced beyond compare! Yes, the Lord was truly with her!

Mary was indeed the servant of the Lord (1:38a). But now, conceiving the Son of God, she would be the Lord's servant in an even more marvelous way (1:38b). "For nothing will be impossible with God" (1:37).

## "Here Am I, the Servant of the Lord" (1:38ab)

The first part of Mary's response, "Here am I, the servant (*doule*) of the Lord" (1:38a), should be seen in relation to Gabriel's greeting: "Greetings (*chaire*, hail), favored one (*kecharitomene*, fully graced one, wondrously graced one)! The Lord is with you" (1:28).

At first, Mary had been greatly troubled by the greeting and pondered what it meant (1:29). Gabriel quieted her fear, showing the relationship between the greeting and her conceiving the Son of the Most High. She had found grace with God in view of her role in the Incarnation (1:30–33). After hearing Gabriel, she was no longer troubled, but she had a question (1:34). Gabriel answered her question. She would conceive the Son of the Most High through the power of the Most High (1:35).

Her question answered, Mary responded to the greeting, showing herself as one fully graced. The Lord was with her. She was the servant of the Lord. The Lord was present to her. In her response, she reflected the Lord's presence back to the Lord. As she would sing in her Magnificat,[1] her response proclaimed, "My soul magnifies the Lord" (1:46).

## "Here Am I" (1:38a)

Mary's response began with the biblical word, "Here am I (*idou*, behold, look, or listen)." With that simple but arresting word, all attention shifts to Mary's response, as she presents herself as "the servant of the Lord."

Gabriel had used the same term, "and now (*kai idou*, behold)" (1:31), shifting attention from Mary's person (1:29) to the Incarnation, the reason she found grace before God (1:31–33). Completing the announcement in answer to Mary's question, Gabriel had used the same expression, "And now (*kai idou*, behold)" shifting attention from Mary's child to be born (1:35) to Elizabeth, who has conceived in her old age (1:36–37). Beginning her response, Mary shifts attention from the angel's announcement to her openness before the Lord.

## "The Servant of the Lord" (1:38b)

Declaring herself "the servant of the Lord (*he doule kyriou*)," Mary placed herself totally at the Lord's disposition. Later, visiting Elizabeth, she again spoke of herself as the servant of the Lord in conjunction with a reference to her lowliness: "for he has looked with favor on the lowliness (*ten tapernosin*) of his servant" (*tes doules autou*, 1:48).

Like many terms, the designation *doulos* (masculine) or *doule* (feminine) had a long and rich history. In the biblical literature, its frequent evocation in the contexts of liturgy, personal prayer, teaching, and simple reading had surrounded it with multiple associations. The word *doulos* (*doule*) was no mere abstraction. It had acquired flesh and blood!

The term *doulos* or *doule* had appeared in the Psalms to describe the Israelite's attitude in the presence of the Lord:

> *Do not turn your servant* (tou doulou sou) *away in anger,*
> *    you who have been my help.*
> *Do not cast me off, do not forsake me,*
> *    O God of my salvation!*
> (*Psalm 27:9; LXX, Psalm 26:9*)

> *Let your face shine upon your servant* (epi ton doulon sou);
> *    save me in your steadfast love.*
> (*Psalm 31:16; LXX, Psalm 30:17*).

> *Remember, O Lord, how your servant* (ton doulon sou)
> *        is taunted;*
> *    how I bear in my bosom the insults of the peoples,*
> *        with which your enemies taunt, O Lord,*
> *    with which they taunted the footsteps*
> *    of your anointed* (tou christou sou).
> (*Psalm 89:50–51; LXX, Psalm 88:51–52*)

> *For he remembered his holy promise,*
> *    and Abraham, his servant* (ton doulon autou).
> (*Psalm 105:42; LXX, Psalm 104:42*)

Like Abraham, Moses was the servant (*doulos*) of the Lord (2 Kings 18:12; LXX, 4 Kings 18:12; see Daniel 9:11), and Moses' lieutenant, "Joshua (*Iesous,* Jesus) son of Nun, the servant of the Lord (*doulos kyriou*), died at the age of one hundred ten years" (LXX, Judges 2:8). Like Abraham, Moses, and Joshua, the prophets were the servants of the Lord: "Surely the Lord God does nothing, without revealing his secrets to his servants (*tous doulous autou*) the prophets" (LXX, Amos 3:7).

Abraham was Israel's great Hebrew ancestor, God's friend, recipient of the promises, and the first in the line of the Fathers of Israel. Moses was the lawgiver, the prophet, the charismatic leader, the creator of Israel's nation, and the mediator of the covenant. Joshua was the military leader, the successor of Moses, the conqueror of Canaan, the agent of covenant renewal, and the guiding presence during Israel's first installation in the land of promise. The prophets were Israel's living faith response to crisis, calling a floundering people to purification and rededication to ideals eroded and strained by external and internal threat, and the human voices of God to his people.

Abraham, Moses, Joshua, and all the prophets were the key figures at major transitional points of biblical history. They were the calibers of God's servants. When the Suffering Servant designated himself the servant of the Lord, he situated himself in their company.

Mary declared herself the servant of the Lord in the company of Abraham, Moses, Joshua, all the prophets, and the Suffering Servant. The designation indicated keen awareness of a new and critical moment in Israelite history. Mary also saw herself as an instrument in the salvation of others.

The four oracles, or songs, of the Suffering Servant (*doulos*) of the Lord are found in the Book of Isaiah (Isaiah 42:1–4; 49:1–7; 50:4–11; 52:13–53:12). [2]

> *And he said to me, "You are my servant* (doulos mou),
> *Israel, in whom I will be glorified"* (Isaiah 49:3).

> *And now the Lord says,*
> *who formed me in the womb*
> *to be his servant* (doulon heauto; *Isaiah 49:5*).

> *The righteous one, my servant, shall make many righteous*
> (*LXX, to justify the just one,* Dikaiosai dikaion,
> *who serves many well,* eu douleuonta pollois),
> *and he shall bear their iniquities.* (*Isaiah 53:11*)

Like the Suffering Servant (*doulos*) of the Lord, Mary is the "servant (*doule*) of the Lord" (1:38b). Describing herself, Mary evoked the prayer of Hannah, who was childless and grieving that the Lord had left her barren (1 Samuel 1:1–8). Here is Hannah's prayer:

> *O Lord of hosts, if only you will look*
> *on the misery* (epi ten tapeinosin) *of your servant*
> (tes doules sou),
> *and remember me, and not forget your servant,*
> *but will give your servant* (te doule) *a male child,*
> *then I will set him before you as a nazirite*
> > *until the day of his death.*
> *He shall drink neither wine nor intoxicants,*
> *and no razor shall touch his head.* (*1:11*)

When Eli the priest saw Hannah praying, moving her lips but making no sounds, he thought she had drunk too much wine. Defending herself, she said her prayer was prompted by her grief and misery, whereupon Eli sent her forth in peace, "Go in peace; the God of Israel grant the petition you have made to him" (1:17). In her response, she again referred to herself as a servant, "Let your servant (*he doule sou*) find favor in your sight" (1:18).

Later Hannah conceived a son and named him Samuel (1:19–20). Samuel grew up to be a great prophet, the one who would anoint first king Saul (10:1) and later David as king of Israel (16:1–13), whose throne Jesus would inherit as the Son of David and the Son of God (Luke 1:32).

Evoking the image of Hannah, Mary's response prepares the reader for her Magnificat, where Mary echoes Hannah's song of praise: "My heart exults in the Lord; my strength is exalted in my God (1 Samuel 2:1).

Mary is the servant of the Lord as Hannah was. But what does it mean to be a servant of the Lord? What, first of all, is a servant? And what did it mean for Mary to be the servant of the Lord?

The Greek word translated as "servant" is *doule*, for which the masculine form is *doulos*.[3] Very often, instead of "handmaid," as in the Revised New American Bible (RNAB), the word *doule* is translated as "servant." For example, the New Revised Standard Version (NRSV) has, "Here am I, the servant of the Lord"; the New Jerusalem Bible (NJB), "You see before you the Lord's servant"; the New International Version (NIV) and the New English Bible (NEB), "I am the Lord's servant." In the New American Standard Bible (NASB) the word *doule* is translated "Behold, the bondslave of the Lord."

The same is found in other parts of the New Testament for both *doule* and *doulos*. The translation of *doule*, for example, in Mary's song of praise, the Magnificat, reads, "For he has looked with favor on the lowliness (*ten tapeinosin*) of his servant (*tes doules*)" (1:48a).[4] The translation for *doulos*, on the other hand, in Simeon's canticle, the Nunc Dimittis, reads, "Master, now you are dismissing your servant (*ton doulon*) in peace, according to your word (*kata ta hrema sou*)" (2:29).

In Peter's discourse on Pentecost, the quotation from Joel 2:28–32 (LXX 3:1–5) reads:

> *Even upon my slaves, both men* (epi tous doulous mou)
> *and women* (epi tas doulas mou),
> *in those days I will pour out my spirit*
> *and they shall prophesy.* (*Acts 2:18; Joel 2:29; LXX, 3:2*)

In the eyes of the Revised New American Bible, therefore, judging from the parallelism between "my servants" and "my handmaids," a "handmaid" refers to a "maidservant," that is, a servant girl or a female servant, in Latin *ancilla*.

The actual Greek word for "servant," however, is not *doule* or *doulos*, but *diakonos*, one who serves at table. By extension, *diakonos*[5] refers to one who is entrusted with all other forms of personal service. The word *doulos* (*doule*) is more properly translated as "a slave."[6] A slave may indeed serve as a servant, but not necessarily. A slave might work on the land, on a building project, or as a galley slave. A servant might be a slave, but he or she might be a free person.

In the New Testament, *diakonia* refers to ministry, and *diakonos* refers to one who is a minister. Unlike *doulos*, the masculine noun *diakonos* has no feminine equivalent. *Diakonos* is used for a female servant as well as for a male servant, for a woman who serves in a ministry as well as for a man.

Most English translations use the term "servant" for both *doulos* (*doule*) and *diakonos*, except when the two are referred to in the same context. A good example of this is found in Mark 10:43–45:

> (43) *But whoever wishes to become great among you*
> *must be your servant* (hymon diakonos);
> (44) *and whoever wishes to be first among you*
> *must be the slave of all* (panton doulos).
> (45a) *For the Son of Man came not to be served*
> (diakonethenai)
> *but to serve* (diakonesai),
> (45b) *and to give his life a ransom for many.*

The example from Mark 10:43–45 shows that *diakonos* and *doulos* are not synonymous and that they need to be translated differently.

In Mark 10:43, "your servant" (*hymon diakonos*) finds a parallel in 10:45a. The Son of Man has come not to be served but to serve (*diakonesai*). Then, in Mark 10:44, "the slave of all" (*panton doulos*) is paralleled by 10:45b, "and to give his life as a ransom for many." That means that the expression "the slave of all" has to be understood as "the slave on behalf of all," that is, as the slave of the Lord, not of the people she or he serves.[7]

Like Jesus, the Christ and the Son of Man, whoever wishes to be first among the disciples gives his life for "the many," that is, for "all." In this context, "the many" is the opposite of "the one" or "the few," and is equivalent to "all."

There is a big difference, then, between *diakonos* and *doulos* (*doule*). As a *diakonos*, servant or minister, a follower of Christ is seen from the point of view of the people to whom he or she ministers. As a *doulos*, a follower of Christ is seen from the point of view of the one in whose name he serves. Christians are *diakonoi* (servants) of the people they serve, but are *douloi* and *doulai* (slaves) of the Lord.

Among the various expressions Paul used to present himself, the term *doulos* (slave) is surely one of the most significant. There are other epithets as well, each of which is an effort to encapsulate verbally the mystery of Paul's person and mission. In Romans 1:1, "Paul, a servant (*doulos*, slave) of Jesus Christ," is followed by two further expressions, "called to be an apostle" and "set apart for the gospel of God."

The self-designation *doulos* does not occur frequently in Paul's correspondence.

In Philippians 1:1, he applied the "servants (*douloi*, slaves) of Christ Jesus" to both himself and his close associate Timothy. On another occasion Paul addressed the Galatians in aggressive self-defense, "Am I now seeking human approval, or God's approval? Or am I trying to please people? If I were still pleasing people, I would not be a servant (*doulos*, slave) of Christ" (Galatians 1:10). In Titus 1:1, Paul called himself "a servant (*doulos*) of God and an apostle of Jesus Christ," in his salutation to Titus, his "loyal child in the faith" (1:4).

The difference between being a *doule* or *doulos* and being a *diakonos* is important for understanding Mary's response to the angel. Mary did not declare herself the *diakonos* of the Lord but the *doule* of the Lord. Mary was not just the "handmaid" of the Lord (RNAB) nor was she simply the "servant" of the Lord (NRSV, NJB, NIV). She was the slave of the Lord.

It is easy to understand why here in reference to Mary's response (1:38), as well as in the Magnificat (1:48), and in most cases where *doulos* is used in the New Testament, translators avoid the word "slave." In English, the term "slave" evokes the horrors of chattel slavery practiced from the very beginning of the colonial era in what is now the United States until well into the nineteenth century. It is hard for us to think of a Christian as a slave, let alone Mary, the mother of the Son of the Most High. But, while understanding why we avoid the word "slave," we must also understand what it means for a Christian and for the virgin Mary to be a *doulos* or *doule* of the Lord.

Mary was the *doule* of the Lord, not of anyone else. Being the slave of the Lord is very different from being the slave of anyone else. Mary was the slave of her Creator. She was the slave of the Lord who sent Gabriel to her, assuring her that she was fully and wondrously graced (*kecharitomene*) and that the Lord (*kyrios*) was with her. The term *kyrios* (lord) is the ordinary correlative of the term *doulos* (slave). Had Mary been the slave of anyone else, she might have had reason to fear, but not as the slave of the Lord. She had found grace with God.

Declaring herself the slave (*doule*) of the Lord, Mary placed herself fully at the Lord's disposition, even as Jesus did as Son of Man and Son of God, even as Christians are challenged to do. Mary denied herself. Instead of claiming herself for her own ends and purposes, she allowed the Lord to claim her for the kingdom of God. Mary, the lowly virgin, accepted to be the mother of God's Son, one who would fulfill the hopes of Israel and extend God's blessing to the whole human race.

Mary's response was very simple but very profound: "Here am I, the servant (*doule*) of the Lord." Her simple words express a wonderful synthesis of the New Testament response to God's invitation and grace. God asked a lot of Mary. Her response included her whole being, challenging every Christian to do the same. In her

Magnificat (1:46–55), she would spell out what that means in terms of salvation history.

Already, Mary's response leaves a lot to ponder. But this was only the first part of her response. The second is just as wonderful.

## "Let It Be with Me according to Your Word" (1:38b)

The first part of Mary's response, "Here I am, the servant (*doule*) of the Lord" (1:38a) was in relation to the angel's greeting, "Greetings (*chaire*, hail), favored one (*kecharitomene*, fully graced)! The Lord is with you" (1:28). Mary had no reason to be troubled or afraid (1:29). She had found grace before God (1:30).

The second part of the response, "Let it be with me according to your word (*to hrema sou*)" (1:38b) was in relation to Gabriel's two-part announcement (1:31–33, 35–37).

*Part One*

> (*1:31*) *"And now,*
>> *you will conceive in your womb and bear a son,*
>> *and you will name him Jesus.*
> (*1:32*) *He will be great and will be called Son of the Most High,*
>> *and the Lord God will give to him the throne of his ancestor David.*
> (*1:33*) *He will reign over the house of Jacob forever,*
>> *and of his kingdom there will be no end."*

*Part Two*

> (*1:35*) *"The Holy Spirit will come upon you,*
>> *and the power of the Most High will overshadow you;*
>> *therefore the child to be born will be holy;*
>> *he will be called Son of God.*
> (*1:36*) *And now,*
>> *your relative Elizabeth in her old age has also conceived a son;*
>> *and this is the sixth month for her who was said to be barren.*
> (*1:37*) *For nothing will be impossible with God."* [8]

The angel ended his announcement, "for nothing (*pan hrema*, every thing) will be impossible with God." The term *hrema* (the word) denotes the reality conveyed by a word. Mary ended her response, "Let it be with me according to your word (*kata to hrema sou*)." She had the last "word (*hrema*)" (1:38b) of the angel's final announcement, "For nothing (*pan hrema*) will be impossible with God" (1:37).

At the end of the first part of the announcement (1:31–33), Mary had a question: "How can this be, since I am a virgin?" (1:34). How could she, a lowly virgin, become the mother of the Son of the Most High? How could she become the mother of a son to whom the Lord God would grant the throne of his ancestor David?

The second part of the announcement (1:35) came in answer to her question. The Holy Spirit would come upon her. Not only would her son be the Davidic Messiah. Conceived in her womb by the Holy Spirit, her Son would the be Son of God.

After the main announcement, the angel also announced that Elizabeth, Mary's relative, had conceived (1:36; see 1:24). After conceiving, Elizabeth had gone into seclusion. Only now was the news made public that she had conceived. And Mary was the first to learn. That Elizabeth conceived in her old age would be a sign for Mary that nothing (*ouk . . . pan hrema*) was impossible with God (1:37).

It was not a matter of Mary conceiving an ordinary human being. Mary was to conceive the Son of God. No human being, including Mary, could conceive the Son of God by having relations with a man. Only God could make that possible through the creative power of the Holy Spirit. Everything (*pan hrema*) was possible for God, including something (*hrema*) that was absolutely impossible for a human being, even for one who was fully graced.

As one who was fully graced, Mary could declare herself the servant (*doule*, slave) of the Lord and accept the message given to her by the angel. But, even as one who was fully graced, she was not able to conceive the Son of the Most High except through the power of the Holy Spirit.

Responding, "Let it be with me according to your word," Mary showed herself ready to receive the Holy Spirit. She placed herself under the power of the Most High that she might conceive and bring forth the Son of God.

The angel Gabriel's statement was that nothing will be impossible for God, more literally, no word (*ouk . . . pan hrema*) will be impossible with God. In her response, Mary professed her faith that no word will be impossible for God, including the word (*hrema*) announced to her.

Gabriel's announcement that no word would be impossible for God referred directly to Elizabeth's pregnancy and indirectly to the announcement to Mary that she would conceive the Son of God. Elizabeth's pregnancy in her old age (*hrema*) was a sign that Mary could conceive the Son of the Most High, not by having relations with a man, but virginally, through the power of the Most High (*hrema*). No word, including Mary's conceiving the Son of God, was impossible for God.

When Mary responded, "Let it be with me according to your word (*hrema*)," she accepted not only the conception and birth of the Son of the Most High, but all that her Son would represent in the world. She accepted her Son's mission, teaching, and ministry, everything that he would do and speak.

With her *fiat* (let it be with me), Mary accepted all that Luke would tell in the Gospel, when he wrote "about all that Jesus did and taught from the beginning until the day when he was taken up to heaven, after giving instructions through the Holy Spirit to the apostles whom he had chosen" (Acts 1:1–2). She accepted also all that Luke would tell in the Book of Acts, showing the apostles as the Lord's "witnesses in Jerusalem, in all Judea and Samaria, and to the ends of the earth" (Acts 1:8).

In her response, Mary was truly the mother of Jesus, one of those "who hear the word of God and do it" (8:21). Given her response, we are not surprised to find Mary, the mother of Jesus, after the Lord's Ascension in the upper room with the Eleven, some other women, and the Lord's brothers, "constantly devoting themselves to prayer" (1:13–14).

## Then the Angel Departed from Her (1:38c)

Having heard Mary's response, the angel Gabriel had completed his mission. Sent from God "to a town (*eis polin,* to a city) in Galilee called Nazareth, to a virgin (*pros parthenon*) engaged to a man whose name was Joseph, of the house of David" (Luke 1:26–27), Gabriel returned to God.

Luke had introduced the encounter very simply: "And he (Gabriel) came to her and said" (1:28a). He concluded the encounter in the same way: "Then the angel departed from her" (1:38c).

With that, the Annunciation to Mary was over. The Annunciation is a story of faith, the faith of Mary, who responded so graciously, and the faith of Christians, who with Luke enter into her story and join with her in faith.

Luke is truly a painter, a painter of icons, one who painted with words. In the New Testament, Luke is the one who painted the first icon of Our Lady, and that icon is the Annunciation to Mary.

---

1.  Robert J. Karris, OFM, "Mary's Magnificat," *The Bible Today* 39/3 (May 2001) 145–149.

2.  For the oracles, songs, or poems of the Suffering Servant, see Carroll Stuhlmueller, CP, "Deutero-Isaiah and Trito-Isaiah," *The New Jerome Biblical Commentary,* eds. Raymond E. Brown, SS, Joseph A. Fitzmyer, SJ, Roland E. Murphy, OCARM (Englewood Cliffs, New Jersey: Prentice Hall, 1990, 1968), 330–331.

3. See Karl Heinrich Rengstorf, "*doulos*," in *Theological Dictionary of the New Testament*, ed. Gerhard Kittel (Grand Rapids: Eerdmans, 1964), 2:261–280; for the institution of slavery, see Muhammad A. Dandamayev, "Slavery," *The Anchor Bible Dictionary* (New York: Doubleday, 1992), 6:58–65 (Ancient Near East and Old Testament), and S. Scott Bartchy, 6:65–73 (Greco-Roman and New Testament); and see Carolyn Osiek and David L. Balch, ch. 7, "Slaves," *Families in the New Testament World* (Louisville: Westminster John Knox Press, 1997), 174–192.

4. The expression is from Hannah's prayer in 1 Samuel 1:11.

5. See Hermann W. Beyer, "*diakoneo, diakonia, diakonos*," in *Theological Dictionary of the New Testament*, ed. Gerhard Kittel (Grand Rapids: Eerdmans, 1964), 2:81–93.

6. For "my slaves" in New Revised Standard Version, see Acts 2:18 (Joel 2:29) and LXX, Joel 3:2, "And on my servants (*epi tous doulous mou*) and on my handmaids (*epi tas doulas*) in those days will I pour out of my Spirit."

7. For servant (*diakonos*) and slave (*doulos/doule*) in Mark 10:41–45, see E. LaVerdiere, *The Beginning of the Gospel, Introducing the Gospel According to Mark* (Collegeville: The Liturgical Press, 1999), 2:115–120.

8. In Greek the very literal translation from "For nothing will be impossible with God" (1:37) is "For (*hoti*) every thing (*pan hrema*) not (*ouk*) will be was impossible (*adynatesei*) with God (*para tou theou*)."

# Conclusion

～

L uke is an historian, a theologian, a superb storyteller, and a person of deep faith. Luke is also an excellent artist. According to Greek Christian tradition, Luke was a painter and he is credited with painting the first icon of Our Lady. Even in the West, medieval artists portrayed Luke as an artist.

Whether Luke painted the icons with pigments on wood, we do not know. But he surely painted with words in the Gospel, and through it on the canvas of the Christian imagination. In his story of the Annunciation to Mary (1:26–38), indeed in each verse, Luke had all five qualities come together—historian, theologian, storyteller, person of faith, and artist.

When the artist El Greco (1541–1614)[1] was nineteen to twenty-five years old, still living in Crete, he painted the Byzantine icon of Saint Luke making an icon of the Virgin Mary and the Christ Child. Luke's icon is the *Hodegetria* (*Hod* = *hodos*, way). The left arm of the Virgin points to her Child, showing the way (*hodos*) to salvation.[2]

As painter of the icon *The Virgin Hodegetria* (or *Hodigitria*), Saint Luke was a patron and protector of Constantinople, and also a patron of artists' guilds in the West from the fourteenth to the sixteenth centuries. Academies of art dedicated to Saint Luke emerged throughout Europe.

I first saw this icon fourteen years ago in San Francisco at the Palace of the Legion of Honor in the exhibition of *Holy Image, Holy Space: Icons and Frescoes from Greece.* I saw it again at the Metropolitan Museum of Art in New York where it was on exhibit from October 2003 to January 2004.

As El Greco saw, Luke was indeed a painter at an easel, applying the last touches to the Virgin's veil. I enter into the icon *Saint Luke Painting the Icon of the Virgin and Child* from the inside. I am sitting beside Saint Luke, applying the finishing touches to the icon. I see the angel descending with a laurel wreath to crown Saint Luke. With the angel, I set the laurel wreath on Luke's head, reading from the scroll, "He created the divine image."

Luke painted with words, inviting us to visualize scene after scene from his Gospel: the Annunciation to Mary (1:26–38), the Visitation (1:39–56), and the birth of Jesus (2:1–20). Luke invited us to visualize scenes from the Acts of the Apostles: the coming of the Holy Spirit (Acts 2:1–13), Saul's conversion and baptism (Acts 9:1–19), and the visions of Cornelius and Peter (Acts 10:1–16). My favorite story in Luke-Acts is the Annunciation to Mary (1:26–38).

While living in Italy (1567–1576) and in Spain (1576–1614), El Greco painted many pictures of *The Annunciation to Mary*. In Venice and Rome, he focused on the angel's greeting and Mary's reaction (1:28–29). Living in Madrid and Toledo, he focused on Mary's response of giving her *fiat* (1:38).

In Venice (1567–1570), El Greco painted *The Modena Triptych*, with *The Annunciation* on the reverse side of the right wing of the triptych. The angel Gabriel is carrying a long stem with three lilies in his left hand. With his right hand, he points to Mary, saying, "Greetings, favored one! The Lord is with you" (1:28). The virgin Mary is sitting at a small wooden table, with her left hand on an open book, probably the Bible. Interrupting her reading, she looks at the angel with perplexity, and lifting her right hand to point to her breast: "But she was much perplexed by his words and pondered what sort of greeting this might be" (1:29).[3]

Living in Rome (1570–1576), El Greco portrayed the same two pictures closer to each other than in *The Modena Triptych*. In the early 1570s,[4] he painted *The Annunciation* with the virgin in her bedchamber, kneeling at a prie-dieu, and in the mid-1570s,[5] Mary is seated at a small table.

In Toledo, about 1597–1600,[6] El Greco painted *The Annunciation*, making larger or smaller replicas on commission. The virgin Mary appears standing and turned toward a lectern with an open book, probably the Bible. She opens her arms, turning her face towards the angel Gabriel. The angel Gabriel, his hands crossed over his breast, is shown venerating and revering the virgin Mary, who looks up expectantly from the lectern, giving her response: "Here am I, the servant of the Lord; let it be with me according to your word" (1:38a). Above, the Holy Spirit as a dove descends in a bolt of light between cherubs' heads. The upper part of the painting is crowned with the glory of the Incarnation, with heavenly angels playing various musical instruments.

In Toledo, El Greco painted a circular image of *The Annunciation* (1603–1605)[7] in the vault over the high altar in the church of the Hospital of Charity at Illescas, a town on the main road between Madrid and Toledo. The virgin Mary kneels at the prie-dieu with an open book. She opens her arms, facing the angel Gabriel. The angel, his arms crossed over his breast, is shown revering the virgin Mary, as she responds with her *fiat*. A dove of the Holy Spirit descends upon her, and the lilies, a symbol of purity, are in a vase on the floor near the prie-dieu.

Sometime between 1608 and 1614, El Greco began his last *Annunciation*, intended for a side altar in the Chapel of the Hospital de San Juan Baptista in Toledo, but it was never completed. He died on April 7, 1614. El Greco's son, Jorge Manual Theotokopoulos, finished *The Annunciation* between 1614 and 1622.

The angel's right hand points to the virgin Mary, and he is probably saying, "The Holy Spirit will come upon you, and the power of the Most High will overshadow you" (1:35a). Mary appears standing, turned away from the prie-dieu, her left hand over a book, probably the Bible, her right hand open toward the angel

Gabriel. She is probably saying, "Here am I, the servant of the Lord; let it be with me according to your word" (1:38a). The Holy Spirit as a dove descends, coming upon her.[8]

I enter into El Greco's many paintings of *The Annunciation* and see them from the inside. My very favorite is the portrayal of *The Annunciation* that he painted about 1597–1600, when he lived in Toledo. In the upper part of the painting, I am among heavenly angels, each one playing a musical instrument in honor of the Incarnation, "And the Word became flesh and lived among us" (John 1:14a). Near the virgin Mary, I say with her, "Here am I, the servant of the Lord" (1:38a).

Luke painted with words the special icon of the Annunciation to Mary (1:26–38), inviting us to enter into the story and meditate on each verse. We will enter from the introduction, "In the sixth month the angel Gabriel was sent by (*apo*, from) God . . ." (1:26–27), and will remain inside through the conclusion, "Then the angel departed from her" (1:38d), returning from Nazareth to God. As such, we will enter into Luke's faith story of the Annunciation to Mary and from the inside contemplate each verse.

*In the sixth month* of Elizabeth's pregnancy with John the Baptist, *the angel Gabriel was sent by* (from) *God* with a divine mission of announcing to Mary the conception of Jesus *to a town* (city) *in Galilee called Nazareth*, an insignificant village in the Galilean hills. As one standing before God, Gabriel had direct access to the throne of God. From his exalted position, Gabriel was sent to Nazareth, a very humble place (1:26).

God sent the angel Gabriel *to a virgin*, who is a lowly person. To be really somebody in biblical culture, a young woman had to be a mother. To be a truly great person, a woman had to have many children, ensuring a great future for her, her husband, her family, indeed, for the people of God. As a virgin, Mary was a lowly person, but she was *engaged* (betrothed) *to a* high *man whose name was Joseph, of the house of David. The virgin's name was Mary.* Luke highlighted

Mary's identity as a virgin, as the one who virginally conceived the Son of God (1:27).

*And he* (the angel Gabriel) *came to her and said, "Greetings, favored one* (fully graced one)! *The Lord is with you."* As "fully graced one," the address to Mary stands in between; it is more than a title, but not quite a name. With the angel Gabriel, we will come to the Virgin Mary and say, "Hail, wonderfully and singularly graced one! The solidarity of the Lord is with you!" (1:28).

*But she* (the virgin Mary) *was much perplexed* and deeply disturbed *by his words.* With Mary, we will be deeply troubled at the absolute awesomeness of what was said. *And* Mary *pondered* (asked herself) *what sort of greeting this might be.* Identifying with Mary, we will ponder the greeting with her, over 2,000 years after the event. Who would not be troubled at such an extraordinary greeting (1:29)?

*The angel said to her, "Do not be afraid, Mary, for you have found favor* (grace) *with God."* Since Mary is fully graced, the Lord is surely with her (1:28). With Gabriel, we will respond to Mary's reaction to Gabriel's greeting. We will begin by reassuring Mary that she has found wonderful grace with God (1:30).

And Gabriel said to her, "*And now* (behold), *you will conceive in your womb and bear a son, and you will name him Jesus."* The announcement includes the elements of her commission. With Gabriel, we will focus on Mary, the virgin of Nazareth, and announce that she will conceive in her womb and bear a son, whom she will name Jesus (1:31).

After focusing on Mary (1:30–31), we will focus entirely on Jesus, announcing to Mary that "*He will be great and will be called the Son of the Most High, and* he will play his divine role in the history of salvation: *the Lord God will give to him the throne of his ancestor David. He will reign over the house of Jacob forever, and of his kingdom there will be no end."* Fulfilling the messianic hopes of the house of Jacob, the house of Israel (Exodus 19:3), Jesus' reign would transcend the house of Jacob. As divine Messiah, Jesus' eternal kingdom would transform the kingdom of David and the house of Jacob into the kingdom of God (Luke 1:32–33).

*Mary said to the angel, "How can this be, since I am a virgin?"* In the story of the Annunciation, Mary is clearly presented as "a virgin engaged to a man whose name was Joseph . . . The virgin's name was Mary" (1:27). Her question, "How can this be?" really asks, "How can I be the mother of the Son of the Most High?" Identifying with Mary, we will also ask, "How can this be?" Conceiving the Son of the Most High has nothing to do with having relations with a man. No human relationship, and no human effort, would enable Mary to conceive the Son of God (1:34).

With the angel Gabriel, we will reply to her question, announcing, *"The Holy Spirit will come upon you."* For Mary to conceive the Son of God, the creative Spirit of God would come upon her. As the Son of the Most High (1:32), *the power of the Most High will overshadow you. Therefore the child to be born will be* great and *holy; he will be called Son of God.* In Jesus' Baptism, "a voice came from heaven, 'You are my Son, the Beloved'" (3:22) and in the Transfiguration, "from the cloud came a voice that said, 'This is my Son, my Chosen'" (9:35).

*"And now* (behold), *your relative in her old age has also conceived a son,"* John the Baptist, the prophetic forerunner of Jesus, the Son of God. *"And this is the sixth month* (1:26) *for her who was said to be barren."* Elizabeth's conception of John in her old age prepared the way for Mary's conception of Jesus as a virgin: *"For nothing will be impossible with God"* (1:36–37).

From the inside, we will hear Mary's response and witness Gabriel's departure. *Then Mary said, "Here am I* (Behold), *the servant* (the slave) *of the Lord; let it be with me according to your word."* Immediately after Mary's response, the Holy Spirit came upon her and the power of the Most High overshadowed her (1:35). Mary virginally conceived in her womb and bore a son (1:31). She conceived "the Word" who "became flesh and lived among us" (John 1:14). With the Virgin Mary (1:27, 34), we are virginal, icons of Jesus Christ our Lord. We are also icons of the Annunciation to Mary (1:38ab).

*Then the angel* Gabriel *departed from her*, returning from Nazareth to the throne of God. Having heard Mary's response, the angel Gabriel had completed his mission (1:38c).

1. El Greco was born in 1541 at Candia (Iraklion), Crete, a Venetian possession. He died on April 7, 1614, at Toledo, Spain.

2. El Greco's proper name is Domenikos Theotokopoulos. He lived in Crete from 1541 to 1566. The young artist, as a Venetian citizen, decided to go to Venice to study. From 1567 to 1570, El Greco studied under Titian in Venice. He is generally known as *El Greco* (the Greek), a name he acquired when he lived in Venice. The definite article *El* (the) may be in the Venetian dialect. From 1570 to 1576, he lived in Rome. In 1576, he moved to Madrid, Spain. The Spanish court had moved from Toledo to Madrid in 1561. From 1577 to 1614, he lived in Toledo, the old capital of Spain.

3. See David Davies, "El Greco's Religious Art: The Illumination and Quickening of the Spirit," *El Greco* ed. David Davies (London: National Gallery Company, 2003), 45–71, esp. 45–47; Fig. 11 (p. 47), *The Modena Triptych* (1568), tempera on panel, side panels 24 x 18 cm.; Galleria Estense in Modena, Italy.

4. See *El Greco*, ed. David Davies (London: National Gallery Company, 2003), 104–105; catalogue no. 12, oil on poplar panel, 26.7 x 20 cm., Museo Nacional del Prado, Madrid.

5. Ibid. 112–113; catalogue no. 16, oil on canvas, 117 x 98 cm., Museo Thyssen-Bornemisza, Madrid.

6. Ibid. 170–171, 16–17, 56–57; catalogue no. 40, oil on canvas, 114 x 67 cm., Museo Thyssen-Bornemisza, Madrid. This picture is a reduced replica of *The Annunciation* (315 x 174 cm.) that was the large altarpiece for the Colegio de Dona Maria de Aragon in Madrid (1596). It is the Museo Nacional del Prado at Madrid.

7. See Richard L. Kagan, "The Toledo of El Greco," pp. 35–147, esp. 106–107; and Alfonso E. Perez Sanchez, "On the Reconstruction of El Greco's Dispersed Altarpieces," trans. Edward J. Sullivan, pp. 148–176, esp. 168–171; in *El Greco of Toledo* (Boston: Little, Brown and Company, 1982), figures 52, p. 106, and 101, p. 170; circular, 50 ³⁄₈ inches in diameter.

8. The upper part, cut long ago from the canvas, the *Concert of Angels* (110.5 x 204.5 cm.) is in Athens, the National Gallery (Pinakothiki)-Alexandros Soutzos Museum. The lower part, *The Annunciation* (294 x 209 cm.) is in Madrid, the Central Hispano Collection. See *El Greco, Identity and Transformation*, ed. Jose Alvarez Lopera (Milan: Skira Editore S.p.A., 1999), 328, 437–438; catalogue nos. 89a and 89b, oil on canvas.

# Index